IN SUCH AN HOUR

DAVID M. GRIFFIS

FOREWARD BY R. LAMAR VEST

Pathway
PRESS

Unless otherwise indicated, scripture quotations are
from the King James Version of the Bible.

Library of Congress Catalog Card Number: 98-66877

ISBN: 0-87148-4447

Copyright © 1998 by Pathway Press

Cleveland, Tennessee 37311

Dedication

To Judy

who chose parsonages, pulpits, and prayer
to walk the road of life with a preacher.

Table of Contents

Foreword

As we approach the dawn of a new century, every tick of the clock brings new and probing questions about the future. There is no shortage of forecasters who tell us they have found the answers, and they are more than willing to share with us the significance of unfolding developments. The truth is, they are engaged in mere speculation. Only the Bible has clear and trustworthy answers.

Unlike the self-proclaimed prophets of today who peddle vague and general predictions, David M. Griffis has probed God's Word for explicit descriptions of end-time conditions without resorting to embellishment or sensationalism. *In Such an Hour* categorizes with extraordinary clarity those events that describe what the Bible calls the "last days." With forthright declaration, the author allows the Bible to speak for itself.

We indeed live in troubled times. The world stage is being set for a spiritual showdown. Christians increasingly have to deal with the rise of a last-days antichrist spirit. More than anything else, we need to hear a clear message from the Lord. David Griffis, once again, has been signally used of the Lord as a messenger. His warnings are clear, but they ring with hope. He writes like a prophet.

Brushing aside the prophetic disclosures that reveal the subtle attacks of Satan could prove fatal. In his 1994 book, *Spirit Wars*, David Griffis opened this challenge to us. Now, he takes us deeper. He uncovers the causes of some of the end-time events and challenges us, while we are looking at the events, to look into our own hearts, which sometimes become the fertile ground for deception.

David Griffis has presented the gospel face-to-face to tens of thousands of people. He is an excellent preacher. He communicates in a unique way. In this book he has done what many speakers attempt but never quite attain. He writes like he speaks, clear and to the point. You don't have to guess what he is trying to say. Let his words help prepare you for these last days.

—Lamar Vest
First Assistant General Overseer
Church of God
Cleveland, Tennessee

Acknowledgements

I want to thank the many people who have helped to make this book a reality. *John Childers*—the assistant general director of Youth and Christian Education for the Church of God, a valuable friend and colleague—has encouraged me all the way. *Tony Lane*, our coordinator of Christian Education, has given sound advice and partnered with me to write the *Instructor's Guide*.

Homer Rhea and his fine editorial staff have been most helpful. *Sam McGraner*, a friend and my personal editor, has been a godsend. *Pat Bradbury* and her staff of marketers have worked tirelessly for the success of this project. *Wayne Slocumb* did a masterful job with the cover design. *Joyce Guiles*, an outstanding Christian and a great secretary, has typed and retyped the manuscript.

The Reverend Garland Griffis, my dad and my favorite preacher, has counseled and offered the advice only a godly father can give. *Dr. Lamar Vest*, my friend and colleague, who wrote the Foreword, was a real source of inspiration. The prophecy preachers and "prophets" of my youth—*Albert Batts, James L. Slay, George Britt, Jack Drake*, and others—stirred within me a longing to know more of God's Word. And finally, my family—my wife, *Judy*; my son, *Jeremy*; and my daughter, *Aubrey*—has filled me with encouragement and love to persevere until this book was done. To all these dear friends, I say, "Thank you!"

CHAPTER 1

The Paradox

Good and bad, darkness and light, righteousness and evil—these are all simple concepts. But as simple as these words are to understand in their relation as opposites to each other, it is amazing that the world has developed a mind-set that clouds these obvious differences. Concepts such as these should quickly be identified as "different," but our age has become the "age of paradox." Many conflicting things are happening in the world today. The onslaught of evil that has covered the globe like a heinous, filthy blanket has caused a blindness to take place in the hearts of men. People are actually doing what God's Word condemns as wrong, and yet they see themselves as doers of good. Like the misguided thinkers of whom the apostle Paul wrote about in Romans, they fall into the category of those who "professing themselves to be wise, they became fools" (1:22).

The deeds of men who cannot distinguish good from evil are a phenomenon of the last days, which we will study in depth as this treatise develops. However, the most obvious paradox of our time is parading itself in front of us with ever-increasing regularity. This paradox is one of the key Biblical signs of the end of the world that God has given in His Word. The amazing thing concerning this paradox is that due to the nature of the two paradoxical elements involved, many people have allowed themselves to be innocently blinded to the true gravity of the situation that now exists. If one can look at both sides of the picture and see what is really going on in the world today, a shocking truth quickly comes into focus.

Before identifying these two elements, let us first look at the word *paradox* itself. According to the dictionary, the word *paradox* means "a seemingly absurd but possibly true statement; a self-contradictory statement." Now, if one takes this definition and applies it to the two obvious spiritual conditions that exist in these last days, one can readily see that we live in a world of spiritual paradox. It is just such an hour as this that will be in existence on the earth when Christ returns and the world is plunged into God's crucible of judgment known as the Tribulation.

Here are the two paradoxical spiritual conditions that the Bible predicted would exist in the last days. On one hand, God's Word teaches that there will be a tremendous outpouring of God's Spirit. The prophet Joel declared emphatically: "And it shall come to pass afterward, that I will pour out my spirit upon all flesh; and your sons and your daughters shall prophesy, your old men shall dream dreams, your young men shall see visions: And also upon the servants and upon the handmaid in those days will I pour out my spirit" (2:28, 29). This last-days outpouring of God's Spirit is a true end-time spiritual event.

On the other hand and on the opposite side of the coin, the Bible says there will be a flood tide of evil—moral and spiritual decay and wickedness that will "abound." It is even prophesied that in the Christian world there will be a "falling away."

It is at this juncture that the serious student of Biblical prophecy pauses in confoundment at the nature of these two prophetic happenings. How can there be both revival and ruin? Should one not counteract the other?

The truth is that these two trends occurring together are like a refiner's fire. It is in this fire that hypocrisy is burned away. Only the sold-out, dedicated Christian who is "in the world but not of the world" (see John 17:11, 16) will be able to stand. The prophet Daniel wrote plainly of this time in the last chapter of his great prophecy. The angel of the Lord told him, "Go thy way, Daniel: for the words are closed up and sealed till the time of the end. Many shall be purified, and made white, and tried; but the wicked shall do wickedly: and none of the wicked shall understand; but the wise shall understand" (12:9, 10).

Let us now consider these two events of spiritual paradox that will signal the end of man's days upon this earth and usher in the new heaven and new earth.

The apostle Peter confirmed the prophecy of Joel on the Day of Pentecost in Acts 2. When the Holy Spirit was poured out upon the 120 in the Upper Room at Jerusalem and the outward manifestation of rejoicing was noised abroad in the city, the Scripture tells us that a great multitude came together. Now it happened that this assembled multitude, according to Acts 2:5-11, was from "every nation under heaven." They were in this crossroads of the ancient world for the religious festivities that were distinctive to the Jewish faith. Once again God's timing was impeccable. When the listeners heard these 120 Galileans speak clearly and distinctly in the languages of the known world, and heard them speak of the wonderful works of God and magnify Him, the Bible simply says that they were "confounded" (v. 6). It was at this point that crowd speculation began to run rampant as to the cause of this spiritual happening. At this point also, the apostle Peter, in verses 16-21, began his powerful and famous discourse by explaining to the multitude that this was the beginning of the fulfillment of Joel's last-days prophecy of a Holy Spirit outpouring.

Since the time of Christ the church has gone through various stages of existence. The time slot of the New Testament itself was a period of spiritual ups and downs. A careful reading of the Book of Acts and successive references, both veiled and clear, reveal that the early church had its high and low moments. Both revival and persecution existed. There was political acceptance, and yet there was bloody martyrdom. There was bold and brash evangelism, and yet there were times of hiding from sworn enemies of Christianity. The church grew and developed until it was a force to be reckoned with. Of course, it was also during this time that the Roman Empire began its foul period of inward decay from which it would never recover. Internal political strife would not be the demise of Rome, but rather Rome's cancerous moral decay would eat away at the fiber of its strength and character. As she weakened, her pompous Caesars, like Caligula and Nero, would search for victims to blame and would find the blood of Christians to their appetite. Unbeknown to these mad despots, however, was the indisputable fact that truth grows best in blood-soaked soil. The early Christian martyrs demonstrated to the world that the cause of Jesus Christ was one that any dedicated follower would gladly die for. The Christian church became firmly established on earth and, every day of her early life, saw Jesus' prophecy at Caesarea Philippi become a living reality. You remember that the Master had spoken in Matthew's Gospel and said, "Upon this rock I will build my church; and the gates of hell shall not prevail against it" (16:18). The early church was established as Christians were soaked in tar, lashed to poles, and burned as human torches to illuminate the streets of Rome. The church grew while Christians became the prey of wild lions and enraged bears, as the elite of Rome's masses laughed in drunken hysteria. The young church of Jesus grew as the followers of the lone Nazarene were sewn up in animal skins with ravenous rodents, and pulled limb from limb between opposing teams of huge horses.

This blood-soaked church would remain strong and evangelistic for many years until the inner decay of ritualism and ecclesiastical trappings would force it into that period of time known as the Dark Ages. For centuries false doctrine and clergy-dominated religion bearing the cognomen of Christianity would exist, and millions would follow false teachings in ignorance and wantonness. The only redeeming thing that can be said about this period of church history, or even about this period of world history, is the fact that the Holy Scriptures were preserved and recorded. The tragedy is that for centuries only the eyes of the elite ecclesiastical hierarchy and the darkened inner sanctums of cloistered monks in remote monasteries would have access to the sacred Word of God.

Perhaps it can be said that the last days began with the great Protestant Reformation and the revival of access to Scripture for all the peoples of the earth. I believe, however, this was simply God's lifting of the veil of darkness as a result of the prayers of hungry people. I do believe that with the Protestant Reformation, God's foundational plan for the last days began. Just look at the multiplicity of things that followed this great event. Though it would be impossible to analyze them in a work such as this, a cursory glance at this period of history allows even the casual reader to see that divine architecture was at work. It was during the month of October in the year 1492 that Christopher Columbus discovered America. It was during the month of October in the year 1517 that the German monk Martin Luther nailed his Ninety-five Theses on the door of the castle church at Wittenberg and began the Protestant Reformation. Exactly 25 years to the month separated these momentous events. Though the world had lain in darkness for a thousand years, it is mesmerizing to see what would take place in the next 400 years. The world would unfold and an entire hemisphere would open to the gospel. Advancements in the arts, science, transportation, medicine, communication, weaponry, and the advent of the modern age would all take place. During this time there would be outpourings of spontaneous revival in various locales, but basically it would be confined to Europe and European-based nations like the United States and Canada. There were isolated instances of revival in Asia and Africa, but these vast regions remained primarily under the influence of paganism. Missionary efforts were sparse and did not increase dramatically until the advent of the 19th century with the proliferation of the British Empire and the Victorian Era. This 400-year awakening of the world was, however, only a dress rehearsal for what was about to take place. The 20th century was about to dawn. God was once again going to fulfill the prophecy of the Hebrew prophet Joel. As the 19th century would close and the 20th century was being birthed, it would happen. The Spirit would fall from heaven.

In rural and mountainous eastern Tennessee and western North Carolina, the Holy Spirit would fall upon a group of lowly mountain people seeking a deeper walk with God. On a street with the odd name of "Azusa" in the city of Los Angeles, a mighty revival of the Holy Spirit would fall that would shake the world. On the plains of Kansas, on the Ozark foothills of Missouri, in the inner cities of large metropolises around the world, in isolated villages of Asia, and in places heretofore unheard of, God began to do a work around the globe. This 20th-century infant Pentecost was at first reviled and rejected by nominal Christianity. But this rejection did not stop or deter its growth in the least. In fact, it toughened its constituents and strengthened their resolve to walk in the power of the Spirit. Today as the 20th century draws to a close, estimates of worldwide Pentecostals range from 200 million to 400 million or more. Even under communist restrictions and severe persecution, it is estimated that there are between 75 million and 100 million Pentecostal believers in mainland China. Seventy-five years of Soviet barbarism and unbelievable persecution did not stop the Pentecostal Movement from growing in Russia. I conducted an interview with an elderly Russian widow whose Pentecostal husband was murdered at her feet by Stalin's henchmen for refusing to disclose the hiding place of his Bible. She then was raped and tortured in front of her children for the same refusal. My interview with her was in the early '90s and her faith had never wavered since that night of horror in the 1930s. During the interview she clutched in her hand the treasured Bible that she would not give up that night so long ago. I talked with an underground pastor in mainland China who had tasted the bitter dregs of prison, hunger, and beatings for his one "crime" of preaching the gospel. I interviewed a pastor from the South Pacific who went to an island of demon worshipers and within a year had a church of 1,500 Spirit-filled believers. Around the world God is doing marvelous things and the outpouring of last-days Pentecost is undeniable. It is happening in every segment of the globe.

It is especially happening among the young. Like the young Israelites who survived 40 years in the wilderness with Joshua, young people around the world are hungry for God's fullness. It's interesting that shackles of materialism or a desire for prestige and protocol do not bind these youth that have been labeled "Generation X." They are genuinely hungry for God. They make up the "sons and daughters" segment of Joel's prophecy, and God is honoring the truth of His Word through them. They fill massive auditoriums for Christian music concerts and youth rallies. They have organized thousands of high school Bible-study clubs and have an annual day of prayer around school flagpoles in addition to conducting daily prayer on campus grounds. They witness in malls and on college campuses and spend their summers ministering to the homeless and destitute both in their native lands and in various mission fields around the globe. They are an army of youth, unheralded by the press and ignored by society's mainstream. They are God's elite and a living fulfillment of Joel 2:28.

While this outpouring of God's Spirit does not get the attention of the worldwide media, there is another element that does. This is the second element of our last-days paradox. Though God did say He would pour out of His Spirit upon all flesh, the same Bible and the same God give us another, equally graphic, prophecy. Let us see what God has to say in His Word about what will happen in the lives of men that is in direct contrast to the outpouring of the Spirit.

In 2 Timothy 3:13, we read these chilling words: "But evil men and seducers shall wax worse and worse, deceiving, and being deceived." What makes this statement so alarming is that Paul had just prefaced these words with the first five verses of the third chapter, in which he warned that "in the last days *perilous* times" would come. He then listed 19 different types of spiritual decay that would invade the hearts of men and women.

Jesus, in His Mount of Olives prophecy, as found in Matthew 24, warns of an evil condition that would hallmark the last days: "And because iniquity shall abound, the love of many shall wax cold" (v.12). Though the Bible contains a number of words that relate the concept of sin, the word *iniquity* is almost exclusively used to denote the sins of the righteous or religious. Could Christ be saying to us that due to the hypocrisy and sinful failures of the religious world in the last days, love will grow callous and goodness would wane? This may very well be the case. John's portrait of the Laodicean church in Revelation 3 is that of a church that declares itself to be rich and increased with goods and has need of nothing. God's answer is that they are wretched, miserable, poor, blind, and naked (v. 17).

Jesus stated that the last days would be like the days of Noah and the days of Lot. Peter wrote of a time of scoffers and people in the church world who would doubt Christ's return even as it is about to happen (2 Peter 3:3, 4). Jude wrote of last-days apostasy and rebellion against godly authority, warning that it would be laced with Satanism and witchcraft. Daniel stated, "The wicked shall do wickedly" (12:10).

You may ask if these two elements can coexist. How can there be revival and an orgy of sin at the same time? The answer is that it is happening now and on a scale such as humanity has never seen. No period of human history can be totally likened to this one. The paradox has arrived. The clock is ticking. A trumpet is ready to sound.

CHAPTER 2

Prophets and
Pinpoints

*Neither have we hearkened unto thy ser-
vants the prophets, which spake in thy
name to our kings, our princes, and our
fathers, and to all the people of the land*
(Daniel 9:6).

Daniel's prayer of intercession in
chapter 9 will forever remain one of the most powerful ones in the history of humanity. It could be equaled
only to the plea of Moses for God's mercy on Israel
(Exodus 32:30-32), or David's cry for forgiveness
in Psalm 51. It is eclipsed only by the prayer of
Jesus in John 17 for the preservation of His disciples. This prayer, of course, was laced with blood

and wrapped in agony, beneath the brittle branches of ancient olive trees in Gethsemane's dark garden.

The thing that stands out so powerfully in Daniel's prayer (see 9:6) is the admission that Israel's fate of captivity by their enemies was the result of their failure to obey the warnings they had received from God's servants, the prophets. He further stated that these prophets had not neglected anyone in their warnings; kings, princes, their fathers, and indeed "all the people of the land" heard these prophetic warnings and simply refused to give heed. And now Daniel pleaded to God for forgiveness for this corporate failure to listen and to act upon what had been prophesied.

A prophet of God is one to be listened to. History is replete with foolish souls who ignored or disdained the words of God's prophets. Bloated, swollen corpses, disintegrating gradually as food for ravenous sharks and fish, testify that Noah's prophecy of a flood was correct and repentance would have been much in order. Sulking Israelites with manacles on their wrists and ankles—exhausted beneath the willows of Babylonian rivers, with no song on their lips— would admit that Jeremiah's pleas were prudent and should have been listened to. A king named Ahab, lying in a pool of thickening blood on the floor of a chariot, with the shaft of a Syrian arrow protruding from a wound in the middle of his armor buckle, would admit that Micaiah, the prophet of the Lord, had been right in his warning (I Kings 22). Ahab's wife, Jezebel, years after Ahab's death, would find herself broken and crushed after a fall from a tower. As a team of chariot horses bore down upon her, bringing horrible death, her mind would know the truth—God's prophet Elijah had been right all along (2 Kings 9).

God has a special relationship with His prophets. As long as they totally obey Him, He places them under divine protection, and they speak as His mouthpiece to humanity. God's warning to those who would harm His prophets is very explicit: "Touch not mine anointed, and do my prophets no harm" (I Chronicles 16:22).

Once God anoints a prophet to speak in His name and the prophecy is given, then the listener becomes responsible for it. Jesus prophesied that Jerusalem would collapse (Matthew 24:2; Luke 21:24). He prophesied that the great Temple would reach such a stage of destruction during the fall of Jerusalem that not one stone of it would be left standing upon another. This prophecy was so hated by the unbelieving Jews who heard it that they used it to rail and mock Him while He died on Calvary. The Scripture says, "And they that passed by reviled him, wagging their heads, and saying, Thou that destroyest the temple, and buildest it in three days, save thyself. If thou be the Son of God, come down from the cross"(Matthew 27:39, 40).

In A.D. 70, 37 years after Christ's death and resurrection, Titus, the Roman military genius, would surround and besiege Jerusalem. The Jews would be savagely butchered by the hundreds of thousands, while survivors would be dispersed as slaves throughout the Roman world. The great Temple would be plundered and the Roman soldiers would tear it down—stone by stone—in search of hidden treasure, and as an affront to the Jewish religion. The ancient historians said they plowed the ground where the Temple had stood, with teams of horses and oxen. Jesus had said it, and it had happened. It must be apparent by now that we must listen with intensity to the words spoken by holy prophets of God.

The Hebrew word for *prophet* is *nabiy* (naw-bee). It means "one who proclaims or relates a message he has received; a herald, announcer, or spokesperson." The word for *prophet* occurs more than 300 times in the Old Testament alone. Though the word can refer to false prophets as well, it was primarily used to refer to prophets of God. False prophets were always identified as such by word or deed.

Prophets came from all walks of life and from every segment of society. God used farmers, herdsmen, scribes, priests, princes, and statesmen. Some prophesied less than a paragraph; others prophesied volumes. According to Jeremiah 1:7, 8, a prophet was not to be afraid or intimidated by his listeners. In fact, God told Ezekiel, "Be not afraid . . . "though briers and thorns be with thee, and thou dost dwell among scorpions: be not afraid of their words, nor be dismayed at their looks, though they be a rebellious house" (Ezekiel 2:6).

The test of a true prophet is found in Deuteronomy 18:22: "When a prophet speaketh in the name of the Lord, if the thing follow not, nor come to pass, that is the thing which the Lord hath not spoken, but the prophet hath spoken it presumptuously: thou shalt not be afraid of him." Prior to this utterance, in verse 20, God declared that false prophets must die. Old Testament law left no room for doubt. False prophets lived short life spans.

God's true prophets, though often disdained, lived to please God and God alone. Though overlooked, the ministry of the prophet is a ministry that God placed in the church and should be active today.

31

It may be that an absence of this ministry, or rejection by individuals to the prophetic call, is a reason for apathy and apostasy rampant in so many last-days congregations. Anointed prophets call men and women to repentance and warn of the consequences of iniquity.

Several prophets of the Old Testament prophesied of conditions, both spiritual and physical, that would exist in the last days. We would do well here to remember the words of the apostle Peter concerning these ancient seers of the Old Testament: "For the prophecy came not in old time by the will of man: but holy men of God spake as they were moved by the Holy Ghost" (2 Peter 1:21). Let us look at a few of these prophecies.

Isaiah. Isaiah's record for accuracy is unblemished. It was Isaiah who first told us that Christ would be born of a virgin (7:14). It was he who prophesied that the Messiah would come as a child, a son (9:6). In the year that King Uzziah died, as the nation lay in the depression of deep mourning, Isaiah saw the Lord, "high and lifted up" (6:1). He foretold the fall of Babylon (ch. 21), the invasion of Jerusalem by the Assyrians (ch.. 22), the folly and failure of Israel in turning to Egypt for alliance (ch. 31), and the destruction of Sennacherib, the king of Assyria (ch. 37). His prayers brought about the prolonging of Hezekiah's life (ch. 38), the angelic destruction of the Assyrian army (37:36-38), and a host of messianic prophecies.

It is in Isaiah 60, however, that we shall turn our attention to some particular last-days prophecies concerning Israel that are specific and mind-boggling. In verse 2, he speaks of a "darkness [that will] cover the earth, and [a] gross darkness [that will cover] the people." He was obviously referring to Israel and the time of their dispersion after the fall of Jerusalem in A.D. 70. It was at this juncture of their history that they were spread to the far-flung reaches of the earth, and as a dispersed and despised people, they lived in Isaiah's prediction of "gross [deep] darkness." While bathed in blood, dragging His cross toward Golgotha, Jesus had foretold the same thing as Isaiah. When He beheld the women bewailing and lamenting Him, He turned to them and said: "Daughters of Jerusalem, weep not for me, but weep for yourselves, and for your children. For, behold, the days are coming, in the which they shall say, Blessed are the barren, and the wombs that never bare, and the paps which never gave suck. Then shall they begin to say to the mountains, Fall on us; and to the hills, Cover us" (Luke 23:28-30). For about 1,000 years after the fall of Jerusalem, the sons and daughters of Abraham suffered "gross darkness." They were despised and rejected, persecuted, and abused. Then the Nazi regime of Hitler's Third Reich attempted genocide upon them, and succeeded in murdering 6 million of these forlorn people.

Notice, however, that in 60:3, Isaiah predicts that "Gentiles shall come to [their] light, and kings to the brightness of [their] rising." It was after World War II that the powerful Gentile nations of the United States and Great Britain stood by Israel as they arose to nationhood once more. Isaiah had prophesied, "Who hath heard such a thing? who hath seen such things? Shall the earth be made to bring forth in one day? or shall a nation be born at once? for as soon as Zion travailed, she brought forth her children" (66:8). It was in one day in the desert of Canaan that Israel formed her government in 1948. The prophecy came to pass.

In Isaiah 60:8, there seems to be a symbolic prophecy of Israel being defended and uplifted by the miracle of flight as the prophet cries, "Who are these that fly as a cloud, and as the doves to their windows?" Any student of modern history is aware that the Israeli air force is arguably one of the finest in the world. The best and brightest are chosen as tender youths to defend the land of Israel in the cock-pits of supersonic jet fighters.

In verses 9 and 10, the prophet talks of for-eign ships and sons of strangers who would bring the dispersed people of Israel back to the shores of their homeland. Some Bible scholars interpret "the ships of Tarshish" (v. 9) as "ships of the islands of tin," which is a reference to the ancient British Isles where the metallic chemical element number 50, or "tin," was mined. If indeed this translation is correct, then the verse pinpoints prophecy even further. It was the British ships that brought the Israelis to their home-lands after lifting their blockade in the late '40s. God's Word is indisputable, and the prophet's pen is sharp.

In verse 12, there is a frightening prophecy that every government on earth should read and take heed to: "For the nation and kingdom that will not serve thee shall perish; yea, these nations shall be utterly wasted." This verse corresponds precisely with what God told Abraham in Genesis 12:3: "And I will bless them that bless thee, and curse him that curseth thee." Over and over again, history has proven this prophecy to be completely correct. This certainty will not diminish, for God has made a promise and His promises are immutable.

These are but a few of the pinpoint prophecies of Isaiah concerning Israel in the last days. Those living today have witnessed much of the fulfillment of this statesman prophet's utterances. We stand in awe at God's ability to fulfill His Word.

Ezekiel. This prophet also pinpointed Israel's restoration in the last days. His prophecy in chapter 37—where he was "carried out in the Spirit of the Lord" and set down in a valley of dry bones—is one of the most unique in Scripture.

Ezekiel was a priest in Israel, which means he was of the tribe of Levi. He was a captive, carried away into the land of Babylon by the Babylonian army. While his fellow captives would mourn and weep and look homeward, Ezekiel would have a powerful experience with God that would cause him to impact his nation, and leave us with numerous last-days prophecies.

In Ezekiel 37, the nation of Israel is portrayed as a valley of skeletal remains after their dispersion. God shows Ezekiel how, by the power of His Spirit, dry bones can come together. Flesh and tissue cover the bones, and as breath fills these beings, they stand on their feet, an exceeding great army.

In verse 11, God tells Ezekiel that these dry bones are "the whole house of Israel," and He recounts their lament of hopelessness: "Our bones are dried, and our hope is lost: we are cut off for our parts." In verse 12, God tells Ezekiel to prophesy and that He would bring them out of their graves and back into the land of Israel. In verse 14, God says He will put His Spirit in them and they will live, and He will place them in their own land. In verses 15-23, He confirms that they will be one nation, not two, and that they will be cleansed forever from the worship of idols.

This prophecy is remarkable. In fact, it describes Israel exactly as it was prior to 1948—spread out and broken, disjointed and hopeless. It took the Spirit of God to unify and join them. In 1948 they became exactly what Ezekiel prophesied—"an exceeding great army" (v. 10). How could a dispersed, scattered people, who had just lost 6 million of its population, unify itself, organize a government, establish a great army, defeat its enemies (though outnumbered by millions), and turn a desert into a garden—except that the Spirit of Almighty God had breathed upon them! So Ezekiel had written it, and so it was done.

Daniel. This prophet is the last of the pinpoint prophets of the Old Testament we shall consider. The entire Book of Daniel is saturated with eschatological substance. Volumes have been written concerning Daniel's visions and the prophecies shown to him by the Divine Architect of history. Therefore, we will concern ourselves with two prophecies in the physical world and two prophecies in the spiritual world that Daniel tells us will pinpoint the last days.

In Daniel 12:4, Daniel is told to cease writing his book and to seal it up "even to the time of the end." Then, in the same verse, God makes one of the most precise and astounding prophetical statements in Scripture. He identifies the "time of the end" as a time when "many shall run to and fro, and knowledge shall be increased." What this literally translates into is a last-days society hallmarked by a noticeable increase in transportation and travel and by a signal increase in knowledge. Was the prophet accurate? Has this come to pass? If he is accurate and this has happened, then my friend, we are a last-days generation. These two prophecies make this undeniable.

Until the turn of the 20th century, transportation was a slow and arduous process. The peoples of the earth, unless their occupation demanded otherwise, basically remained in their sphere of living unless emergencies arose. Horse-drawn carriages and wagons, steam locomotives, and ships provided the bulk of movement. Speeds were slow with maximums in the 35-mile-per-hour range. This had been the case for centuries—then something happened. Almost overnight there was the internal combustion engine, automobiles, diesel-powered ships, airplanes, and mass transit. Today the pace is breathtaking. The billions of earth's populace travel constantly. One can breakfast in Paris, take a seat on a Concorde jet, lunch in New York, board a commercial airliner, and partake of dinner in a fashionable restaurant in Los Angeles. Men spend days in space on space stations, fly shuttles into space to launch satellites that orbit our planet, while dispensing a myriad of information. Cars fill our interstate-highway systems by the millions. In other parts of the earth, the story is the same as crowded byways are filled with an active, constantly moving humanity.

How could a Hebrew prophet, thousands of years ago, have even imagined such a time? The human mind of Daniel's day was not culturally trained to even think in these terms. But it didn't have to be, for God revealed it to him. God—whose eyes see past, present, and future—knew this condition of constant travel and motion would exist in the last days. Thus, He told His prophet Daniel, who told us under the anointing of the Holy Ghost. This sign alone should make us tremble, but another solidifies it even more.

God said through Daniel that "knowledge" would increase. Scholars have said that from the time of Christ until the year 1800, the accumulated knowledge of man doubled once. It is said to have doubled again from 1800 until the turn of the century. What had originally taken 1,800 years to occur, now occurred in 100 years. Then, from 1900 until 1920, shortly after World War I, it is said to have doubled again. And so the trend has continued—knowledge doubling within 20 years, then 10 years, then five, and now as often as every year and a half. What is taking place? Atoms, computers, microbes, cloning, lasers, virtual reality—everything the mind can even begin to imagine is happening in the world of knowledge. Much of what has happened had to happen to fulfill the Scripture concerning the rise and rule of the Antichrist, which we will discuss later. Can this be a coincidence? I think not!

Daniel's prophecy about the increase of knowledge in the end time is upon us now. No other period of human history can point to a time comparable in the slightest to this one. Though there has been an occasional renaissance in culture, the arts, or science, the explosion of knowledge in the late 20th century is a mind-boggling phenomenon.

As if these two physical pinpoint prophesies were not enough, Daniel then gives us two spiritual prophecies to further pinpoint the end of time.

In 12:10, Daniel simply is told by God that "many shall be purified, and made white, and tried; but the wicked shall do wickedly: and none of the wicked shall understand; but the wise shall understand."

Notice two things that happen to the righteous in the last days. First, they are "purified." This is a cleansing act of God's power. This has to occur for them to be raptured. Jesus said emphatically, "Blessed are the pure in heart: for they shall see God" (Matthew 5:8). The psalmist said the man who would "ascend into the hill of the Lord" would be the man who had "clean hands, and a pure heart" (Psalm 24:3, 4). This prophecy seems to indicate there will be a revival of purity and holiness prior to the coming of the Lord. What a necessity! Second, Daniel also says that they will be "made white." This has to do with identification in a saint's life. Notice that when the saints are portrayed on white horses in Revelation 19:14, they are clothed in "fine linen, white and clean." The white linen is identified in verse 8 as "the righteousness of saints." God will identify His

41

people by their righteousness in the last days. This is not a "self-righteousness," for that kind of righteousness is as "filthy rags"; but this righteousness comes from a purified, clean heart that is wholly spiritual, in tune with God's precepts, and trained by God's Word.

Daniel's second spiritual prophecy is in total opposition to the first. He states that "the wicked shall do wickedly" (12:10). You might ask, Has this not always been so? But the thing Daniel speaks of here is a different degree of evil. It's as if he is saying that though people are identified as "wicked" by their wicked deeds, in this end-of-the-world time their wickedness will go beyond the normal progression of evil. The idea here is something totally satanic in nature, evil on a scale never before seen or heard of. Only the people in the days of Noah and Lot could have experienced evil on this kind of scale, and God destroyed them. In fact, this powerful verse ends with the haunting statement, "None of the wicked shall understand; but the wise shall understand." May we ask wisdom of God to understand just exactly what lies ahead.

CHAPTER 3

"As It Was . . .
So Shall It Be"

But as the days of Noe were, so shall also the coming of the Son of man be (Matthew 24:37).

Likewise also as it was in the days of Lot; they did eat, they drank, they bought, they sold, they planted, they builded; but the same day that Lot went out of Sodom it rained fire and brimstone from heaven, and destroyed them all. Even thus shall it be in the day when the Son of man is revealed (Luke 17:28-30).

The return of Christ, the Great Tribulation period, and God's final judgment are futuristic events that constitute the culmination of a period known as the last days. Though Jesus was emphatic in His statement that no man would know "the day or the hour" (see Matthew 24:37; 25:13) that the Son of Man would return, He did give many indicators as to what the time would be like when He returned.

The most precise indicators are the two periods of ancient Biblical history that occurred during the lifetimes of Noah and Lot. Though each of these men lived centuries apart, the events surrounding the cataclysmic time in each of their lives was very similar. The events that took place during their times, which literally brought about the destruction of their worlds, are events that are both spiritual and physical. By this we mean that the physical manifestations that prompted God's judgment upon the worlds of Noah and Lot were brought about by spiritual conditions of human hearts that had drifted far from God.

In both instances, the worlds of Noah and Lot became repulsive to a holy God, who judged them swiftly and completely, though He extended mercy and warning beforehand. It is also interesting to note that each case of judgment was caused by opposing forces of nature. Noah's world was destroyed by the devastation of limitless water, and Lot's world was engulfed by incendiary heat. The results were the same. A pitiful few righteous individuals were saved and the overwhelming majority was destroyed. The Biblical record is clear, and several races of the descendants of both men inhabit the planet today. Scientific and archeological evidence abounds which indicates both events happened exactly as the Scripture said. The aftermath is left for us to analyze and then with a solemn soberness, to give heed to the warning of Jesus. His phrase, "As it was . . . so shall it be" (Luke 17:26, 28) must occupy our thinking as we compare current events to the events that existed in the days of both Noah and Lot. It just may be that the Savior gave us His most urgent warning. One must conclude, after reading the words of Jesus, that this prophecy of Noah and Lot comes closer to actual date setting than anything found in the pages of Holy Writ. What happened then is happening now with frightful regularity. The spiritual barrenness of those days is mirrored in the bankrupt hearts of men and women today. The physical manifestations of homosexuality, lesbianism, perverse sexual practices, obsession with materialism, humanistic thinking, and even land and building development, are reminiscent of those days of ancient yesteryear. In that day the anger of an awesome, all-seeing God was kindled and

He roared out His wrath in unprecedented proportions.

Let us now examine these two periods of history and attempt to decipher just what it was that so angered the Lord. As we do, may our eyes wander to the late 20th century and see if the "So shall it be" part of Jesus' prophecy is being fulfilled.

Noah. Since Noah lived first, he and his age will receive our first scrutiny. We are first introduced to the man Noah in Genesis 5. We are told he was the son of a man named Lamech and the grandson of Methuselah. Methuselah is famous as the man who lived a longer life span than any other—969 years. It is interesting to note that Methuselah's name translates, "And when he is gone, then it will come" (according to Finis J. Dake). Noah's father, Lamech, died when he was 777 years old, exactly five years before the Flood took place. However, Lamech's father and Noah's grandfather, Methuselah, lived five years longer than Lamech, dying the year the Flood came. This is a Scriptural fact and now we understand that Methuselah's name is a prophetic one. This is made clearer when we understand that Methuselah's father was Enoch, whom Jude identifies as a prophet who prophesied the return of Christ to earth (Jude 14, 15). Enoch never died but was translated into the presence of God (Genesis 5:24). He begot Methuselah when he was 65 years old and gave him the name that meant "And when he is gone, then it will come." Methuselah's death meant that the Flood was imminent. Enoch was a true prophet of God.

Noah lived in a day of great strife in the earth. It was during his day that God stopped the long life spans of men as a tool of judgment and gave them a life span of 120 years. At the same time, He also announced,"My spirit shall not always strive with man" (Genesis 6:3). This is our first indication of God's anger being heated toward the men of Noah's day. This was a portent of things to come.

A revelation is given to the reader of Genesis 6, a revelation so frightening in its implications that any man who fears God is taken aback upon reading it. In verse 5, God observes wickedness on a scale He has never observed before. He describes this wickedness as "great." This wickedness was generated by the fact that every imagination of the thoughts of men's hearts was continually evil. Verse 6 is saturated with sadness, as we view the heart and mind of God at work: "And it repented the Lord that he had made man on the earth, and it grieved him at his heart." Here a saddened and brokenhearted God is found wishing that He had never created His finest creation. Sin had produced bitter fruit, and as that fruit ripened then rotted, the stench was nauseating to a holy and righteous God.

God's decision is awesome and terrible to consider. "And the Lord said, I will destroy man whom I have created from the face of the earth; both man, and beast, and the creeping thing, and the fowls of the air; for it repenteth me that I have made them" (v. 7). Never has one who sat upon a bench in judgment issued a more terrible decree. The complete annihilation of life from the planet Earth is a decree of judgment like no other in the history of the universe. It would be over. No flock of geese would ever make their V across the skies. No chorus of frogs would sing their summer night song from the marsh. No gazelle would ever again leap in graceful flight. And no child's smile would ever light up in wonder at the beauty of a butterfly. A mother would never again cry with joy at the sight of a wet, wrinkled newborn babe, and no man would feel the pride of work well done. Sin had at last destroyed it all. The decision had been reached. Destruction was imminent and sure. Soon only chemical elements would remain where a globe of life had once encircled the sun in its God-directed orbit. But something happened.

Genesis 6:8 is one of the most important verses in all of Holy Writ. This verse stands prominently between the destruction of life and the mercy of God on the earth. It simply reads, "But Noah found grace in the eyes of the Lord."

One man—like a brilliant diamond on a piece of black velvet, and like a burning candle in the darkest of nights—had gotten God's attention with his righteousness. God would destroy the earth and all the wickedness in it, but He would spare the human race and the animal life of earth, because he found in Noah a truly righteous man.

Let us look at some things that existed in Noah's day that brought life to the brink of destruction. These are the same things that Jesus said would exist in the end times. These things are so obvious, and are on such an intense scale, that there will be no doubt in the minds of the observer—if they are found on the earth today, then we are living in that period of time Jesus prophesied about.

The first obvious thing that marked Noah's day was the great wickedness that filled the earth. Since there has always been evil since the fall in Eden's Garden, one is made to wonder just how bad it must have gotten in Noah's day for God to consider the total extermination of mankind. Genesis 6:11-13 offers us some insight: "The earth also was corrupt before God, and the earth was filled with violence.... All flesh had corrupted his way upon the earth.... The earth [was] filled with violence through them." According to Webster's, the word *corrupt* carries the following meanings: "dishonest; open to bribery; debased; evil; tainted; perverted; injured; impure." Such was the nature of mankind in Noah's day. God said they imagined and thought continually about evil (v. 5). It's interesting to note here that God is concerned about our thoughts and the course of our thinking. The Scripture says, "For as he thinketh in his heart, so is he" (Proverbs 23:7).

Noah's day must have been a day of perverse thinking, political corruption, and bribery. Scandals must have abounded, and the lives of men and women were surely tainted and corrupted with licentiousness. Dishonesty was a way of life, and to "fit in" such a society many would adapt themselves to these corrupt ways. In such a society the abnormal becomes the normal. That which is an abomination becomes accepted as rational behavior. It doesn't take long in the kind of society that Noah lived in for the righteous to become despised and for those who herald the truth to be labeled fanatics. Does any of this sound familiar? When one reads about Noah's day, it seems as if history is repeating itself in our day. Should this surprise us? Did not Jesus say, "As it was . . . so shall it be?"

Another area of wickedness that stood out in Noah's day was the intense atmosphere and arena of violence. This blood lust was so prevalent that God mentioned it twice in chapter 6.

Violence is spawned from spiritually depraved conditions like hatred, frustration, anger, jealousy, and revenge. Each of these conditions develop in lives out of touch with God. Men and women in touch with God and His laws shun and avoid feelings that develop into violence. Since Noah's day was characterized with rampant violence, so it will be in the end of time. A last-days earth will be an earth that is corrupted with violence.

When the headlines of modern newspapers are replete with stories of murder, assault, maiming, and suicide—that society is filled with violence. When family members settle their disputes with guns and knives, and when battered, beaten spouses and children seek refuge in state-run shelters—that society is corrupted with violence. When children and teenagers carry murderous weapons to school and use them

51

to steal leather jackets and athletic shoes, that society is corrupted with violence. When prisons bulge with overcrowding, when pornography is a multibillion-dollar-a-year business, when mayhem and bloodletting fill the streets of inner cities—we have mirrored the days of Noah. God is "no respecter of persons" or ages. If God was repulsed by the violence of Noah's day, so God's anger must be kindled in such an hour as this.

There is another reason for this violence that will be discussed in another chapter at length, but it is important to mention here. Last-days violence is a part of the antichrist spirit that is growing and rapidly covering the whole earth. Violence can be seen in Northern Ireland, throughout the Middle East, in the developing nations of Africa, the drug-infested valleys and highlands of South America, the capitals of Europe, the dysfunctional nations of the former Soviet Union, China, and Southeastern Asia. Every major metropolis of the globe has demographic sections within its geography where violence, crime, and the occult rule and dominate. The evil spirits behind this violence is in direct contrast to the gentle teachings of the lone Nazarene.

The media of our day, especially the movie and music industry, has capitalized on the spirit of violence. The most popular of Hollywood's flicks run rivers of blood and splatter the silver screen with broken bodies and lifeless corpses. Modern music has mesmerized the youth culture with everything from satanic "death metal" music to "gangsta rap." Singers cry for blood, death, illicit and violent sex, and the suicide of the listener. Does not the Biblical word *corrupted* of Genesis 6:12 have to apply here? The spirit of antichrist that the apostle John warned us about in 1 John 4:3 is manifesting itself today in the form of violence.

When John the Revelator saw the vision of the four apocalyptic horsemen in Revelation 6, each horseman represented a stage of the Antichrist's reign on the earth during the Tribulation period. The four horses were white, red, black, and "pale" (or gray). Each stage is marked with a type of violence. The Antichrist enters history's stage on a white horse promising peace, but note carefully there is a bow—an instrument of death, if you will—in his hand. He goes forth to conquer (v. 2). The next time he is seen, he is on a red horse and he is armed with a great sword (v. 4). He is given power to take peace from the earth and to cause men to kill one another. Next he is seen upon a black horse. He bears scales and casts famine and hopelessness upon the earth (vv. 5, 6). This can create nothing but further violence. The final horseman is called Death, and Hell follows him. He has no goal but worldwide violence. One-fourth of the earth are now killed with the sword, hunger, death, and the beasts of the earth (v. 8).

It may be that the violence of this hour is but a dress rehearsal for the Tribulation period. Certainly at the very least, it is a signal warning to us that we have become like the people of Noah's hour and the Lord's return is imminent.

Another thing that is noteworthy about Noah's day was the fact that they were busy with everyday living to such an extent that they had no time for God-consciousness. Jesus said "they were eating and drinking, marrying and giving in marriage, until the day that Noe entered into the ark, and knew not until the flood came, and took them all away; so shall also the coming of the Son of man be" (Matthew 24:38, 39).

What an indictment of a generation! To live as if this world would be the only world they would ever have demonstrates the height of spiritual foolishness.

This possessiveness with everyday existence and no eye on eternity was without excuse in Noah's day. The Bible referred to Noah as a preacher of righteousness. In 2 Peter 2:5, the apostle of Pentecost declared, "[God] spared not the old world, but saved Noah the eighth person, a preacher of righteousness, bringing in the flood upon the world of the ungodly." The people of Noah's day were warned of this impending tragedy. Noah preached righteousness. The very act of his building an ark had to draw attention and arouse curiosity, but it was without effect. Jesus said they lived as if one day would bring about another day and were unaware of the approaching watery doom until it became a reality.

Today the gospel is preached and the cries of warning are heard. However, the desire to live as always occupies the attention of earth's populace, and the cry to make ready for eternity is seldom heeded. "As it was . . . so shall it be."

Lot. According to Jesus, history's other great lesson teacher is the Biblical character known as Lot. He was the nephew of Abraham. Much of his life was spent observing his righteous uncle, and under his tutelage Lot must have learned something of the ways of God. The apostle Peter tells us that Lot was both just and righteous (2 Peter 2:7, 8). We do know that God was willing to send two mighty angels into the dwelling place of Lot on the eve of Sodom and Gomorrah's destruction (Genesis 19).

Lot's life will be remembered tragically, however, as a man who could not convey his righteous principles to his family or his city. Though spared from the destruction of Sodom and Gomorrah, our last glimpse of him is that of a drunken widower, incestuously fathering the nations of Moab and Ammon by his own two daughters. Both nations would plague Israel forever.

What were the days of Lot in Sodom and Gomorrah like? What would cause Jesus to say, "As it was in the days of Lot . . ." (Luke 17:28)?

First of all, God said that "the cry of Sodom and Gomorrah is great, and . . . their sin is very grievous" (Genesis 18:20). In verse 32, God indicated that He would not destroy the cities if there could be found as many as 10 righteous people in all of Sodom and Gomorrah. Genesis 19:1-10, tells us that men of the city, both young and old, from every quarter of the city, were involved in the sin of homosexuality. The two angels who came to rescue Lot and his family from the imminent destruction were assailed by these sexual deviants. These vile men of the city tried to force Lot to send the angels out so they could rape and abuse them sexually. Genesis 13:13 states, "But the men of Sodom were wicked and sinners before the Lord exceedingly." Peter said that the men of Sodom were ungodly, filthy in their conversation, and unlawful in their deeds (see 2 Peter 2:5-8). Jude stated that Sodom and Gomorrah were "giving themselves over to fornication, and going after strange flesh" (Jude 7). He also states that they suffered the vengeance of eternal fire. The term *sodomite* is used five times in Scripture; in each usage it denotes those given over to homosexuality, and in each instance God is condemning the practice as sinful and an abomination to the Lord (Deuteronomy 23:17; I Kings 14:24; 15:12; 22:46; 2 Kings 23:7).

It would seem from all references in the Scriptures to Sodom and Gomorrah that there was great sexual perversion and obsessiveness in the land. The lust of the flesh on this scale denotes demonic activity of the worst sort. Unlawful, sexual perversion is often a doorway for demonic work in the lives of individuals.

In Lot's day, God destroyed Sodom and Gomorrah instantly with a storm of fire and brimstone. Abraham would lift up his eyes and look out on the plain the next day and would see smoke that resembled that of a great furnace (Genesis 19:28).

During the latter years of the 20th century there has been a concerted effort in the worlds of entertainment and the media to portray deviant sexual practices such as homosexuality, lesbianism, voyeurism, fornication, and adultery as being acceptable and normal. Those who oppose these trends are decried as religious fanatics and prudish in their behavior. On television and radio talk shows, sinful lifestyles are discussed and accepted with reckless abandon. Laws are passed in state legislatures and in church conferences that place approval on these things that God so openly condemns. One has to wonder how the same God, who overthrew Sodom and Gomorrah and reduced them to sulfuric ash, feels about the world's attitude toward these practices today. One thing is sure. God said, "As it was . . . so shall it be."

The second thing of note in Lot's day, which was also found in Noah's day, was the obsession with life as usual. In fact, according to Scripture there was a fascination with the economy that seemed to prevail. Jesus said that in Lot's day "they did eat, they drank, they bought, they sold, they planted and they builded" (Luke 17:28). Here we see a portrait of economic prosperity and boom. This finely tuned economic machine was satisfying to the inhabitants of Sodom and Gomorrah. It gave them a feeling of unabashed security. Just like people today who vote for wicked and licentious politicians, as long as the economy is good, so the Sodomites rested and reclined in their beds of economic ease and practiced their sin freely. Their philosophy was that a full belly, a good roof, and a sack of gold meant all was well. However, these same people were still well fed, well clothed and economically prosperous when their skin burst with boiling blisters while the stench of their burning hair and clothes filled their nostrils. These "economically happy people" saw their beds of lust incinerated by chunks of fire and brimstone and who screamed with blackened lungs of terror as God said that's enough.

Jesus said judgment came the same day of their ease and at the time of their feeling of security. He also said, "As it was . . . so shall it be."

CHAPTER 4

Perilous Times

This know also, that in the last days perilous times shall come. For men shall be lovers of their own selves, covetous, boasters, proud, blasphemers, disobedient to parents, unthankful, unholy, without natural affection, trucebreakers, false accusers, incontinent, fierce, despisers of those that are good, traitors, heady, highminded, lovers of pleasures more than lovers of God; having a form of godliness, but denying the power thereof: from such turn away" (2 Timothy 3:1-5).

The apostle Paul, dean of New Testament writers, although known for his plain and candid speech, could not have been plainer than he is in his analysis of the last days in 2 Timothy. The first thing that he shares with us in this passage is the warning about what kind of days will unfold in the last days. He uses the word *perilous* which simply means "dangerous." This correlates with Jesus' statements about the last days being like those of Noah and Lot. The question naturally arises: Dangerous for whom? The answer unfolds clearly—these days are dangerous for all humanity. Adverse spiritual conditions will began to develop, and men will take on certain characteristics that will turn them into dangerous human beings. If the peoples of the earth become dangerous, then it stands to reason that the earth they inhabit is also dangerous. The danger is not only physical—though that will abound—but more than anything, this danger is spiritual in nature.

Most often we think of danger in physical terms, but if we think Biblically, we understand that the body is a temporary and fleeting part of our lives. It is the soul that lives on and never dies. That is why Jesus said in Mark 8:36, "For what shall it profit a man, if he shall gain the whole world, and lose his own soul?" According to Jesus, the soul of a man is invaluable. The wealth of the whole world cannot buy or purchase a man's soul. With this in mind, one begins to see that the spiritual dangers that destroy the soul are more deadly than weapons of mass destruction. This is why Christ said, "Fear not them which kill the body, but are not able to kill the soul: but rather fear him which is able to destroy both soul and body in hell" (Matthew 10:28).

Paul's list of deadly spiritual conditions that will destroy men's souls in the last days cries out the word *danger*. While many students of last-days Bible prophecy search for current events and physical signs that point to the imminent return of Christ, no more graphic signs of Christ return exist than these. Paul lists 19 last-days spiritual conditions in 2 Timothy 3:1-5. Each deserves close inspection.

Lovers of their own selves. Only one word is needed here for translation, and that is *selfishness.* There are leading psychologists of our day who speculate that the major social problem of the hour can be boiled down to selfishness. What a selfish time we live in. The most crowded sections of many bookstores are filled with books on self-help, self-improvement, self-searching, and how to love yourself.

The problem with selfishness is that it is the opposite of what Christianity is all about. This makes it an anti-Christ spirit. Jesus said that one of the first steps in discipleship was self-denial. In Mark

8:34, He very plainly stated, "Whosoever will come after me, let him deny himself, and take up his cross and follow me."

How can one love the Lord his God with all of his heart, mind, soul, and strength and love himself first? How can one love his neighbor as himself, if he is so possessed with himself that he can think of no one else?

If one peeled back the facade behind the greed, crime, dirty politics, broken marriages, shattered lives and dreams, the ugly and frightening face of selfishness would appear. The desire to please oneself is as old as Eden and the original sin. Notice the elements in Eve's conversation with the serpent. The subtle serpent appealed to Eve's vision of herself. He told her she would not die as God said. He told her that her eyes would be opened; that she would be as a god; and that she would for the first time really know both good and evil. Selfishness was born here. She wanted vision, the nature of a god and wisdom for herself. God's commands were forgotten as she reached for the fruit. Horror descended upon the human race.

Men's love for themselves in the last days supercedes their love for God and quickly obliterates things like kindness, generosity, and compassion.

This is manifested in rage driving on our highways, manipulation for position in the workplace, unjustified indebtedness for the accumulation of things, and the rise to power at all costs. Selfishness is a last-days trademark that is burning like a prairie fire in a stiff wind. Only a heart submitted to God and sold out to Christ can avoid this vice-grip spirit of the last days.

Covetous. This is in direct violation of the 10th commandment given in Exodus 20:17. Another word for this is *greed*—the desire to have and accumulate. We have almost built the last-days economy on this vice alone and the breaking of the 10th commandment. This generation has gone far beyond the boundaries of working to provide the basic needs of life with occasional pleasures acquired to fragrant our existence. A greedy and covetous spirit has gripped our age. Jesus taught giving, even stating that "it is more blessed to give than to receive" (Acts 20:35).

Our major holidays—Christmas, Valentine's Day, Easter and even Thanksgiving—have taken on huge commercial and materialistic ramifications. Competition among friends, relatives, and neighbors for material status culminates in finer homes, more expensive automobiles, state-of-the-art technological playthings, and exotic trips of leisure. We want and we strive to fill our wants. This can degenerate into financial corruption and even criminal activity. It affects the elite of society and the very poorest of the populace. Clergymen have been known to compromise their integrity. Politicians have cast their honesty aside for the love of money. No wonder Paul stated, "For the love of money is the root of all evil: which while some have coveted after, they have erred from the faith, and pierced themselves through with many sorrows" (I Timothy 6:10).

Boasters, proud, heady, and high-minded. These four last-days evils we shall group together, for they all are similar in nature and represent only different manifestations of a single spiritual degenerative condition. Primarily these conditions are spawned in the human heart as a result of pride. Pride is the oldest of all sins, for it is the soil from which the iniquity and rebellion grew in the heart of Lucifer when he rose up against God before time was. God hates "a proud look" (Proverbs 6:17). This thing called pride cries out by its very existence and says, "I am self-sufficient and I don't need God or anyone else." According to Isaiah 14 and Ezekiel 28, Satan was so full of pride he felt he could ascend into heaven above

God's throne and rule in equality with or even above God. His effort was as short-lived as it was foolish. Isaiah said he was "cut down to the ground" (14:12). Ezekiel said he was "cast . . . as profane out of the [holy] mountain of God" (28:16). Jesus said, "I beheld Satan as lightning fall from heaven" (Luke 10:18).

And now in the last days these same spiritual cancers of pride, conceit, arrogance, and boasting are arising again. Paul said they would occur and signal the time of the end. Nowhere are they more evident than in the sports and entertainment industries. Here competition abounds and riches run like rivers of gold. We idolize men and women for their deeds of daring and skill. We marvel at their beauty and wonder at their abilities. We as a generation worship the stars and starlets, the players and athletes as if they were the gods of Olympus. Pride, boasting and arrogance spill over into the mind-set of our young as we teach them that adulation of these superpeople is acceptable. Kids grow up with a superstar syndrome to deal with. This contradicts the nature of Christ who has said, "He that is greatest among you shall be your servant" (Matthew 23:11). Servants are not filled with pride, nor do they waste their time with boasting. How can one be arrogant and conceited when he has humbled himself to help? Of all the portraits of Christ in the Scripture, none touches our hearts more than the one found in John Chapter 13. See the Carpenter from Nazareth as He girds Himself with a towel, takes a basin of water, and begins to wash the feet of His disciples. His knees are bent, His back is arched, He is lowly and meek of heart, and He performs His task with joy and willingness. This portrait is far removed from this generation that is scarred with pride, boasting, arrogance, and conceit.

Blasphemers. Paul's list of last-days characteristics touches every gamut of this last-days world. When he says they will be "blasphemers," he uses the Greek word *blasphemos*, which means "to speak evil of; to rail, revile, defame, or slander." It is most often used to refer to those who attribute to Satan the works of the Holy Spirit. When done maliciously or with knowledge, it is unforgivable according to Jesus (Matthew 12:31).

Disobedient to parents. This last-days sign of spiritual danger especially appears unique. This phrase must have an expanded meaning by its very nature. Since the dawn of time obedient children were the result of godly parents, and indeed, obedient children most often became godly parents themselves later in life. The first commandment with promise found in Scripture stated, "Honour thy father and thy mother: that thy days may be long upon the land which the Lord thy God hath given thee" (Exodus 20:12).

Satan has attacked the whole family structure in these last days. He hates it for it is God's first institution. God uses the bride-and-groom concept to illustrate Jesus' relationship to the church (Ephesians 5:25-27). Believers are referred to as "children" and the Lord loves us as a father loves his children (I John 4:4; Psalms 103:13). There is a jealousy and bitterness in the heart of Satan toward the relationship God has with His children; and since God has ordained the family structure, Satan has made it a chief last-days target. He has riddled it with divorce, infidelity, violence, financial hardship, and sorrow. He has brought drugs, illicit entertainment, pornography, alcohol, and unbridled materialism into the home. Shattered lives, marred hopes, and devastated homes are the result of his attack. Modern television has distorted the family roles, transforming the father from the priest and head of his home to an unethical dupe like Homer Simpson. Children are taught that "normalcy" can be anything and that there is no perversion or wrong. Many children are

69

taught to be their own person to the point that they don't have to do anything they don't want to do—no rules, no structure, no compliance or conformity. They are given a distorted freedom that if left unchecked leads to anarchy. The prophecy of Paul is clear and visible. Not only are they disobedient to parents, but this hour is filled with parents who teach disobedience by their own rebellion against God.

Unthankful. Paul's list of spiritual last-days signs in 2 Timothy goes on to talk of ingratitude. When he says men will be "unthankful," he is warning of a sense of attitude that cries out and says, "I deserve what I get, it is due me, why should I be thankful." Part of the reason for the spirit of ingratitude in these last days is due to the fact that people have so much. Surprises don't surprise them, and the biggest quandary on special occasions is knowing what to get someone. The gift is then soon forgotten, for we are a generation possessed with the "accumulation" syndrome.

Unholy. Rampant sin and the acceptance of it as part of life brings about a state of unholiness. What once pricked the conscience now is brushed aside and callousness is built around the heart and becomes the order of the day. The apostle Peter says that Lot saw these identical conditions every day in

Sodom and his righteous soul was "vexed" (2 Peter 2:7, 8). When Paul predicts that the last days will be "unholy" in 2 Timothy 3:2, he uses the Greek word *anosios,* which means "wicked; without piety or reverence." What is denoted here is that men will not possess those pious qualities that holy men possess. Their lack of reverence for holy things speaks plainly of their lack of fear for God. This characteristic is very evident in our society. Men live as if they will never face God in judgment. The prediction of Ecclesiastes 12:13-14 is far from their thoughts. The wise man's cry is one that this generation would do well to give heed to: "Let us hear the conclusion of the whole matter: Fear God and keep his commandments: for this is the whole duty of man. For God shall bring every work into judgment, with every secret thing, whether it be good, or whether it be evil."

Without natural affection. Paul prophesies of an unusual condition that will exist in the hearts of many last-days men and women. In 2 Timothy 3:3 he states that men will be without "natural affection." The Greek word used here is "*astorgos,*" which literally means the "affection and love that comes naturally," like the parent's love for the child and the child's love for the parent. In Matthew 24:12 Jesus said, "Because iniquity shall abound the love of many shall wax cold." One has only to observe the enormous increase in our day of physical, sexual, and verbal child abuse to understand the fulfillment of this Scripture. Likewise, stories abound today of children murdering parents and siblings. Men and women have allowed lust to replace true love and eroticism has become an idol god of this age. This is all in total contradiction to God's command in I John 4:7 where we are told, "Beloved, let us love one another: for love is of God." An absence of genuine love and natural affection is a signal sign of the end of time.

Trucebreakers. Paul also states they will be "trucebreakers," a word derived from the Greek word *aspondos*, which means literally, "one who cannot be trusted." This is seen in every segment of society where the bonds of trust that once bound men together have been slashed asunder by greed and avarice.

False accusers. Paul prophesies that men will become "false accusers," which comes from the Greek word *diabolos* and is the same word used to identify devils. It literally means "a slanderer, a spreader of lies and untruths." In the Old Testament the term "sons of Belial" was often used to mean the same thing. Anywhere "sons of Belial" are mentioned they are found lying and spreading falsehood, rumor and innuendo about innocent people. They promote pompous, arrogant leaders like Ahab, when they lie on innocent men like Naboth, when Ahab and Jezebel used them to steal Naboth's vineyard and have him murdered (1 Kings 21). God always deals with them and with those wolves they promote, as He did with Ahab and Jezebel (1 Kings 22; 2 Kings 9).

Our day is beset with false accusers. From biased news reporting to tabloid journalism, we live in a world that thrives on hearing the sensational. Even in the religious world such prevaricators of the truth abound. They are "feet that [are] swift to spread mischief" (Proverbs 6:18) who can't wait to tell the rest of their church world the latest gossip. They want to make sure their spin on things overshadows all others, even if the real truth is sacrificed by their personal "news" organization. They are fed and inspired by "itching ears" and people of small spiritual stature who delight in hearing the "latest." Sometimes these "sons of Belial" have the audacity to spread their rumors and reports in the name of keeping people informed. They envision themselves as a God-called network of ecclesiastical information, never admitting or accepting the malicious damage they have done to the body of Christ. As David slew the man who delighted in bringing the news of Saul's death, so God will deal with those who delight in the mischief of gossip (see 2 Samuel 1:1-16; Proverbs 6:16-19).

Incontinent. Paul continues his list by stating that they will be "incontinent," a word translated from the Greek word *akrates*, which means "having no control of appetites and passions." How very obvious this is in our day of excess.

Fierce. This term comes from the Greek word *anemeros*, which means "savage and uncivilized." In our society we will pay men millions of dollars to stand in a boxing ring and bash each other's brains out, while little children and families live in cardboard boxes and sleep in the dead of winter on sewer grates for warmth. Such a society is slipping rapidly toward uncivilized barbarism.

Despisers of those that are good. The apostle says they will despise "those who are good." This is the only place in the New Testament where the Greek word *aphilagathos* (despisers) is used, and it simply means "very unfriendly to good men." In our only-the-strong-survive society, often men and women with the qualities of goodness, kindness, compassion, and mercy are disdained as weak. This attitude Paul said would be prevalent. The righteous would not be liked in the last days. Jesus said that the world would hate

His disciples because it hated him (John 15:18, 19; 17:14).

Traitors. Paul warns of "traitors," which means "betrayers or turncoats." Loyalty will by no means be an abundant quality in the lives of last-days men.

Lovers of pleasures more than lovers of God. Paul declares that the dangerous world of the last days would love pleasure more than it loves God. There is no need for expounding here. Paul says it all. Enough said.

Having a form of godliness, but denying the power thereof. He concludes his discourse by stating that there would be rampant hypocrisy. This will be discussed at length in chapters 6 and 8 of this work.

CHAPTER 5

Defining Deception

Knowing this first, that there shall come in the last days scoffers, walking after their own lusts, and saying, Where is the promise of his coming?
(2 Peter 3:3, 4).

Deception is not a device of recent invention. It is an old, carefully forged, intricately shaped and sharpened weapon of Satan that has been in existence for thousands of years. Indeed, it was the weapon of choice for the serpent in the Garden of Eden when the Evil One had his first contact with the human race. It worked in the garden with such effectiveness,

that Adam and Eve lay spiritually dead in their tres-
passes and sins, while the corruption of humanity
was ensured.

Deception is a tool of flexibility that works
on a wide range of target areas. The eyes can be
deceived through visual deception. In Genesis 3:6,
the Bible says that the forbidden fruit Eve saw was
"pleasant to the eyes." Natural instincts can be deceived, for in the same verse, Eve was made to believe
that the deadly fruit was "good for food." The idea
relayed here is that Eve's perfectly natural instinct to
eat what was good for the health of the body was
totally and completely convinced that this fruit would
nourish the flesh. Notice also in this same passage
that the mind or thinking process can be deceived.
Eve believed, according to Genesis 3:6, that if she
ate of the forbidden fruit she would be made wise.
This was not a thought she had developed in her
perfectly normal and uncorrupted brain, but she had
allowed her mind to receive seeds of deception like a
fertile field. The Serpent had told her that if she ate
the fruit, she would be as a god with the knowledge
and wisdom of a god (v. 5). Of course, as at the end
of all satanic deception, both Adam and Eve realized
the promises were lies and that horrible consequences
would now have to be reaped. Their realization was

immediate and their judgment was quick. However, with the passage of time we now understand that the realization of one's deception does not always come quickly, nor does the judgment that follows it. But regardless of the time element between deception, conviction, and judgment, the process is sure to take place, and that is precisely what we must understand when we study the deception that will take place in the last days.

The prophecy found in 2 Peter 3 concerning the deception that is to occur in the last days is one of the most important prophecies in the New Testament concerning last-days events. This is truly a spiritual sign of the last days, for it is a condition that will exist within the mind and in the heart. The result of this deception will be that people in the religious and in the secular world will live as if Christ will never return. They will live as if time itself has no end, and as if the cycle of human life and existence will go on forever and ever. Because of this, men will lose their fear of God and their sense of eternity. It will not take long for them to develop an attitude of atheism, as if there is no God and all of life is right now. It's easy to see the consequences of such thinking. In fact if we look at our world as it is now, we can see these consequences unfolding. The prophecy of Peter is in the very act of fulfillment as you are now reading. Let us look closely at the word this Galilean fisherman had received from the Lord.

Simon Peter, a native of the fishing village of Bethsaida, on the Sea of Galilee, was one of the original 12 disciples of Jesus. One of the most unique and colorful characters of the New Testament, he became a powerful leader and preacher in the early church. He had many unique experiences. It was he who once walked on the water to go to Jesus (Matthew 14:27-31). It was he who so powerfully identified Jesus as the Messiah the Son of God, at Caesarea Philippi (Matthew 16:13-20). He beheld Christ on the Mount of Transfiguration (Matthew 17:1-8). These were highlights in Peter's life. But there was also a downside, illustrating his weak humanity and tendency to err in his flesh. In the last hours before Christ's crucifixion, it was Simon Peter, in a fit of temper, who took a sword and cut off the ear of a man named Malchus, a servant of the high priest (John 18:10). No doubt, Peter's intent here was to cleave the man's skull in defense of his Lord. However, God prevented this and Jesus healed the man (Luke 22:51). Had Peter's murderous attempt been successful, he too might have suffered execution, but

God had better things in store for him. Later on that very night, Peter would deny knowing Jesus (Luke 22:54-62). He would end the night with bitter weeping. It is from that moment that we see better things begin to take place in the life of Peter. Christ would tell him after the Resurrection that true love for Christ means that he would "feed my sheep" (John 21:15-17). On the Day of Pentecost, Peter was the evangelist, who not only explained the outpouring of the Holy Spirit as a fulfillment of Old Testament Scripture, but he also preached a powerful message of the saviorhood of Christ. Three thousand souls were added to the church in one day (Acts 2).

Most Bible scholars believe Peter's two epistles were written between A.D. 60 and 65, approximately 30 years after the ascension of Christ. Written to the dispersed Jewish Christians of his day who dwelt throughout parts of Asia Minor, the books of 1 and 2 Peter deal much with the suffering and martyrdom they must undergo as followers of Christ. He mentions suffering 16 times in the first epistle alone.

In his second epistle, however, he begins to deal with last-days apostasy, and a powerful prophetical warning is given. There is a great similarity between 2 Peter and the books of 2 Thessalonians, 1 and 2 Timothy, Jude, and Revelation. It is as if

God was moving in the hearts of Peter, Paul, Jude, and John with a special message of warning to last-days Christians. The theme of a great falling away, deception, callousness, apathy, and backsliding runs rampant through each of these books. It is Peter, however, who deals with a specific last-days spirit of deception. Any serious student of the last days must analyze Peter's prophecy.

In 2 Peter 3:1, 2 he explains to us his purpose in what he is about to share. He says he wants to "stir up" our minds by causing us to remember what the ancient prophets and the New Testament apostles had written. Since deception is a last-days theme dealt with by both Old Testament prophets and New Testament apostles, what comes next is not surprising, but it is alarmingly specific.

He is specific at first about when his prophecy will take place. In verse 3 he states that what he is about to prophesy will happen "in the last days." It is now pinpointed. What he is about to say will take place in the end of time.

According to Peter, scoffers are going to come in the last days. *To scoff* means "to jeer, taunt, deride, and speak sarcastically about something in order to lessen or discredit it." To be a scoffer is bad enough, but the scoffers Peter speaks of here have another problem. They are very self-centered and self-focused. He uses the expression "walking after their own lusts" (v. 3). This means they have their own agenda and it is one of self-fulfillment and self-gratification. They care about things other than God, primarily the lust of their own flesh. Like King Ahab who wanted Naboth's vineyard even if it meant murder, so the generation of scoffers who exist in the last days are motivated by an ends-justifies-the-means type of mentality. Their ethics are situational and not Biblical. Their only world is the present; they do not think of eternity and even deny the supernatural. This of course is the basic premise of secular humanism, which gets its doctrine from the Greek philosopher Protagoras, who taught that "man is the measure of all things." The secular humanist "walks after his own lusts."

The tragedy is that in this prophecy of Peter, he intimates that these scoffers are part of the religious "Christian" world. Their very willingness to discuss end-time events and the coming of the Lord indicates that they are religious people. One can only speculate as to why they have become scoffers, but one thing is made clear that aids us in this speculation—they are observers of the world around them. They have developed an intellectual capacity to observe the continuation of history. They say to themselves and others that since the death of the ancients, everything in the cycle of life just keeps repeating itself and time goes on and on and on (v. 4). They have closed their minds to the possibility of the miraculous and do not believe that Christ will return. They may even believe, somewhat, in the miracles of the Bible and in the way that God moved in the past. Now in the last days, since all the prophets, apostles, and patriarchs are dead, they believe the day of the miraculous is over. They have developed a cold, aloof, intellectual last-days form of Christianity that has no miraculous power of supernatural demonstration in it. They have become scoffers, who demean those who believe in the second return of Christ. They resent the teaching, for they themselves want control of the future development of the church and society. The teaching of the "catching away of the church"—the Rapture—interrupts their plans and makes people dependent on God instead of on themselves and the world of perfection they wish to create. They are self-centered, walking after their own lusts, creating their own empires and little kingdoms on this earth.

According to Peter, their chief tactic is a tool of discouragement to the believer in the Rapture. A simple question suffices for them: "Where is the promise of his coming?" Of course the only answer is the obvious: He has not returned as yet. But it is as this question is being answered that these scoffers begin to justify their scoffing and cynicism. They look to the natural world and talk of life's natural process of continuation. Their view of life is totally humanistic. They would state, "We're born, we live, we die, and the same will be true for our descendants." It is in thinking like this that there is horrible danger. For those who rule out eternity and the sure judgments of God, there is an open path to do what is right in their own eyes. They surmise that if this is the only world they will ever live in, then they can do as they wish to make it as profitable as they can. Therefore, we have people doing things in the realm of Christianity—in the name of God, in the name of the church—but the results they seek are for their own self-advancement. To achieve great religious and humanitarian things for one's own legacy misses the point of Christianity altogether. To do things for God and not know God is an exercise in futility. These types of individuals are all together too numerous in the religious world today. Christ predicted they would exist. In Matthew 7:22, He told of the future judgment when men would boast

85

of their religious deeds done in His name. His answer to them is chilling: "And then will I profess unto them, I never knew you: depart from me, ye that work iniquity" (v. 23). Works, regardless of their value and grandeur, are empty without the virtues of love and faith. Scoffers walk after their own lusts; and men, who seek their own wills, become scoffers. They are quick to "despise those that are good" and make fun of the holy (see 2 Timothy 3:2-5). This is a great veil of deception they pull down over the eyes of their followers, and in Peter's prophecy he gives us keen insight to the fallacy of their viewpoint.

First of all Peter says "they willingly are ignorant" (2 Peter 3:5). This means they do not want to know the truth. Jesus said, "Ye shall know the truth, and the truth shall make you free" (John 8:32). Without truth all men are in bondage. God's Word is truth (17:17). When Peter states that last-days scoffers would be willingly ignorant, he is talking of men who do not want freedom from their bondage. They choose to not know the truth. These are the same last-days men Paul wrote about to the church at Thessalonica. He said these last-days anti-Christian scoffers would be sent a "strong delusion" from God, and they would believe a lie and be damned because they "believed not the truth, but had pleasure in

86

unrighteousness" (2 Thessalonians 2:11, 12). The word for *delusion* here has one simple meaning: "deception." It is a fact of Scripture that those who seek to deceive others are themselves deceived.

Peter says that the deception that enshrouds these scoffers is their lack of understanding concerning the certainty of God's judgment. He uses the example of the flood of Noah's day to prove his point. He says it was by God's express command that the world prior to the Flood existed in a safe and habitable state. Notice his wording: "By the word of God the heavens were of old, and the earth standing out of the water and in the water" (2 Peter 3:5). Then he reminds the reader that judgment came swiftly in the form of the great Flood: "Whereby the world that then was, being overflowed with water, perished" (v. 6). Peter, the evangelist, is saying that one day there was a perfectly normal world that owed its state of existence to the will of God. But on the next day that same world perished in a watery grave because of the declared judgment of God. What a warning for last-days readers! But the apostle of Pentecost does not stop here. His lesson on the surety of God's justice is just beginning. He tells the reader that the world that now exists does so by the same will and word of God. "But the heavens and the earth, which are now, by the same word are kept in store, reserved unto fire against the day of judgment and perdition of ungodly men" (v. 7). Judgment will again come to the earth, Peter says, and this time it will be in the form of fire. Just as in Noah's day, this will be a judgment of ungodly men. And just as in Noah's day, this judgment is sure to happen.

It is at this point that the scoffers say, "But it's not happened yet." They reiterate the fact that Peter's prophecy occurred over 1900 years ago and the earth still remains. Peter anticipated this type of intellectual cynicism, and under the anointing of the Holy Spirit, he dealt with it as skillful as an expert surgeon with scalpel in hand.

Peter explains to the listener that God does not view time as man views time: "But, beloved, be not ignorant of this one thing, that one day is with the Lord as a thousand years, and a thousand years as one day" (2 Peter 3:8). To God there is no difference in a day of 24 hours or a millennium of a thousand years. God is beyond and above time. We on earth measure time by the rotations of our planet and its journeys around the sun. The God who inhabits eternity has no such restrictions. In other words, Peter is saying, "Let's get the right perspective here." Time does not dictate to God. God is the architect and designer of history. John said it so beautifully: "All things were made by him; and without him was not any thing made that was made" (John 1:3).

Peter then uses this premise to defend the surety of God's promises: "The Lord is not slack concerning his promise, as some men count slackness" (2 Peter 3:9). God does not renege on His word. Jesus said, "Thy word is truth" (John 17:17). The prophet declared, "God is not a man, that he should lie" (Numbers 23:19). Paul's cry was, "Yea, let God be true, but every man a liar" (Romans 3:4). The Bible is replete with the truth that what God says He will do, He will do. It is this undeniable fact that Peter is grasping firmly. God will keep His promise, yet God is abundant in His long-suffering and mercy. It is the ending of 2 Peter 3:9 that people should understand in its Biblical context, lest they think that God will withhold His judgment out of His abundant mercy.

Peter emphatically states that God doesn't want anyone to perish. Of course He doesn't. This is why John 3:16 came from the lips of Jesus: "For God so loved the world, that he gave his only begotten Son, that whosoever believeth in him should not perish, but have everlasting life." It's important to see here that the "whosoever believeth in him" must occur before the "should not perish" can take place. The same can be said of Peter's prophecy. God doesn't want anyone to perish, but there must first be an "all should come to repentance" (2 Peter 3:9).

It is in verse 10 that the crux of this entire prophecy is summed up in 14 awesome words of powerful proclamation: "But the day of the Lord will come as a thief in the night." What is the great apostle saying? Can we fathom the urgency of this message?

It's both simple and yet profound: Christ is coming. The Day of the Lord will happen. Judgment in the form of fire will occur, melting the very elements. The earth will be purged. Nothing can stop it. God's great open door for repentance will finally close, as He has declared, "My spirit will not always strive with man" (Genesis 6:3).

As a thief in the darkest of nights slips in unawares and unannounced, so the Day of the Lord will come suddenly. The sword of the Spirit will shred deception's cruel cloak of blindness, and willingly blinded spiritual eyes will shudder in the horror of judgment.

Today is the day of mercy. Tomorrow, the darkness comes.

CHAPTER 6

Jesus and the Tares

As therefore the tares are gathered and burned in the fire; so shall it be in the end of this world. The Son of man shall send forth his angels, and they shall gather out of his kingdom all things that offend, and them which do iniquity; and shall cast them into a furnace of fire: there shall be wailing and gnashing of teeth. Then shall the righteous shine forth as the sun in the kingdom of their Father. Who hath ears to hear, let him hear" (Matthew 13:40-43).

The greatest teacher ever to teach a lesson was Jesus of Nazareth. His teaching changed humanity forever. In fact, His impact upon the earth through His teaching was so powerful that time itself is categorized as being either before Christ or after Christ.

Of course, because He was the Son of God and was divine as well as human, God could teach man personally. But even greater than this obvious fact was the fact that now this God-Teacher had experienced the human condition. This God-Teacher had gone through the birth canal of His virgin mother, on a darkened night, inside a stable in the ancient village of Bethlehem. He had nursed at His mother's breast, stumbled as He learned to walk, explored as a toddler, climbed trees as a little boy, experienced the changes of puberty, learned the carpenter's trade, and knew the responsibilities of manhood. God had become man in the person of Jesus Christ and had not lost His divinity in the process. Paul's exclamation to Timothy expresses it best: "And without controversy great is the mystery of godliness: God was manifest in the flesh, justified in the Spirit, seen of angels, preached unto the Gentiles, believed on in the world, received up into glory" (I Timothy 3:16).

Watch the omnipotent God of heaven with His wisdom, foreknowledge, and an intricate understanding of all things earthly and heavenly as He sits down on a stone and communicates truth to eager listeners. This is a portrait of the perfect classroom.

When you add a loving and compassionate heart and a sense of urgency to this portrait of teaching, then the lesson affects not only the mind but the spirit as well. So it is with the lessons taught by Jesus.

Jesus used the things of His day that the people were most familiar with. The people of ancient Galilee were agrarian by definition. They were rural people, people of the land. Farmers, fishermen, craftsmen, shopkeepers, and dwellers in small villages and hamlets made up His listeners. The land and all that it contained allowed them to live. Drought, blight, locusts, hail, and floods meant hunger. Sunshine, gentle rains, and good seasons meant times of plenty. The skills and ingenuity of these people were familiar to Jesus. He grew up in a land where all participated in the agrarian way of life and were interdependent upon each other. It was because of His intimate knowledge of the ways of life in the ancient Middle East that He was able to teach lessons that were easily understood. He used things people were familiar with to teach profound truth. Their hearts were touched because of the word pictures He painted so graphically. Listeners could easily place themselves in the picture being painted, for they had seen what He talked about and He always made His truth so obvious. Their reactions to the lesson depended upon the condition of their hearts. Some received Him joyfully, while others rejected Him with scorn.

The amazing thing about the parables of Jesus is their agelessness. Though our society has changed, the simplicity of these parables remains remarkably understandable. The complexity and technology of our times do nothing to diminish the lessons taught by Jesus. In fact, the truth that emerges from these lessons, when it is prophetical in nature, is extremely relevant to our times. As with all Scripture, these lessons from the Great Teacher are inspired of the Holy Spirit. What we have here is not just a parable from an ancient wise man; what we have is the infallible Word of the living God. Jesus declared the immutability of His words in Matthew 24:35: "Heaven and earth shall pass away, but my words shall not pass away."

Among the most poignant end-time parables that Jesus taught was the parable concerning the wheat and the tares, found in Matthew 13:24-30:

> Another parable put he forth unto them, saying, The kingdom of heaven is likened unto a man which sowed good seed in his field: but while men slept, his enemy came and sowed tares among the wheat, and went

his way. But when the blade was sprung up, and brought forth fruit, then appeared the tares also. So the servants of the house-holder came and said unto him, Sir, didst not thou sow good seed in thy field? From whence then hath it tares? He said unto them, An enemy hath done this. The ser-vants said unto him, Wilt thou then that we go and gather them up? But he said, Nay; lest while ye gather up the tares, ye root up also the wheat with them. Let both grow together until the harvest: and in the time of harvest I will say to the reapers, Gather ye together first the tares, and bind them in bundles to burn them: but gather the wheat into my barn.

In verse 36 of this same chapter, the disciples asked Jesus to explain this parable of the tares. With-out any reservation Jesus plainly and completely ex-plained the parable (vv. 37-43). He identified the sower of the seed as the "Son of man." He said the field is the world, the good seed are the children of the Kingdom, and the tares are the children of the Wicked One. The "enemy" who sowed the tares is plainly stated as being the devil. "The harvest," Jesus said, is the "end of the world," and the reapers are the angels. He stated what shall happen to the wicked: "The Son of man shall send forth his angels, and they shall gather out of his kingdom all things that offend, and them which do iniquity; and shall cast them into a furnace of fire: there shall be wailing and gnashing of teeth" (vv. 41, 42).

He concludes the defining of the parable by telling them, "Then shall the righteous shine forth as the sun in the kingdom of their Father. Who hath ears to hear, let him hear" (v. 43).

What message is this powerful word drama from the lips of Jesus sending to us today? First, Jesus Christ is sowing the gospel in the hearts of willing recipients. These children of the Kingdom are what Jesus referred to as the "good seed." The "tares" that are intermingled with the good seed are children of the Wicked One that he has sown in the same ground that the good seed is in.

It was a common practice in the ancient East, and it is still practiced today, for enemies to sow tares and other poisonous weeds in the fields of those they wished to hurt. In some lands of the Orient, these unwanted weeds get such a grip on tillable land that it takes years for the farmer to get rid of them.

The Greek word for *tares* that is used here is *zizanion,* which was a grain that looks like wheat while growing but, when full-grown and ripe, has ears which are long and the grains are black and poisonous.

Jesus was saying that in the church world there are those who grow like the tares. They resemble the real thing insomuch that to deal with them would involve the risk of hurting the real thing. Like tares that resemble wheat, their cunning hypocrisy fools all but the eye of the most skilled and spiritual observer. But like the tares at the end of the growing season, their real substance becomes noticeable. God says not to worry about them because He will deal with them at the end of the growing season. "Let both grow together until the harvest: and in the time of harvest I will say to the reapers, Gather ye together first the tares, and bind them in bundles to burn them: but gather the wheat into my barn" (Matthew 13:30).

This is a parable about carefully hidden religious hypocrisy as represented by the tares. The Enemy places these tares in fields that should be producing only wheat. When ripened, wheat is golden, symbolizing its value. Wheat provides the substance for bread, which sustains life for those who partake. Wheat can be preserved until ready for use. Wheat produces more wheat as wheat seeds are sown. Wheat production provides honest labor and the breath of the wind to separate the golden kernel from the useless chaff. Wheat represents all that is good and useful and is a welcome reward to the farmer who has labored to produce it.

The true children of God have the same traits as wheat. They are children of value, and the measure of their value is inestimable. The children of God share the Bread of Life with each other and with other hungry souls who desire to be fed. Prayer, faith, love, and the Word preserve the children of God, even as leaven and salt preserve wheat bread. As wheat makes its own seed to produce more wheat, so the children of God produce more children of God and the Kingdom is constantly enlarged. As the wind separates useful kernels from useless chaff, so the breath of the Holy Spirit blows away the useless things in our lives until we stand totally useful before God, and our lives bring nourishment to the body of Christ. A finished and productive child of God is ample reward for the true servant of God who has labored to plant, water, and till the life God has given him.

As wheat is a blessing to the body of Christ, so tares are a horrible detriment. Tares take up space best used for growing wheat. Tares steal nutrients and water from the soil that could nurture a beneficial crop like wheat. If tares are mistaken for wheat, and if an attempt is made to use them like wheat, then sickness or death to the innocent can occur. The end of the tare is nothing less than an end of total destruction. They are burned up in the fire.

The last-days religious hypocrites that permeate our Christian society are remarkably well represented by the tares in Matthew 13.

Like the tares, they occupy space in the fertile fields of God's church. They drain from churches the time, resources, pastoral attention, and evangelistic fervor that could best be used for winning and discipling the sincere and hungry. When these religious hypocrites are mistaken for real children of God and an attempt is made to give them positions of responsibility or to listen to their counsel or advice, often the results can be deadly. While in the natural world one would not think of eating a poisonous plant, in the spiritual world there is often no effort made to discern between the good and the evil.

This parable of the wheat and the tares comes with an awesome last-days warning. Verse 40 says that "in the end of this world" a final judgment will occur which will settle all doubts as to the wheat and the tares. It's very simple. The "tares," or the hypocrites, are to be gathered and burned in a "furnace of fire." There will be no mercy given or considered.

Jesus had much to say about religious hypocrisy. In this parable of the wheat and the tares, He said that hypocrites "offend" and "do iniquity" (v. 41). This simply means that they hurt the body of Christ by their behavior and that their sins are in the category of "iniquity." Though the Bible has many words for *sin*, when it uses the word *iniquity* it is almost always referring to the sins of the religious.

A listing of religious sins that offend and hurt the body of Christ is too numerous to mention here, but a few Bible examples should give us the gist of what "tare" sins are all about.

One hypocritical sin Jesus denounced had to do with inward rottenness. Jesus compared the Pharisees to cups and saucers that were clean on the outside but inside they were full of extortion and excess (see Matthew 23:25-28). Can you imagine being thirsty and reaching for a clean glass to fill with clear, cold water, only to find the inside full of scum and slime and all manner of putrid matter? So it is with hypocrisy in the eyes of God. As such, a glass is useless for quenching a thirst; such an inward corrupted vessel is useless for Kingdom work.

The "tare" sin of the uncontrolled tongue is offensive to the body of Christ and poison to Kingdom mentality. Proverbs 6:16-19 tells of seven things that God hates—things that are an abomination to Him. Of these seven, four have to do with the tongue. In verse17, God hates "a lying tongue." Regardless of the position and prestige of some religious figures, God says if they lie, He hates their lying tongues. This sin is rampant in the religious world today. Lies, when believed, can do much damage and harm to the church Jesus died for. With the modern-day acceleration of the media, the Enemy has many available means to spread lies throughout the religious world. The printed page, television, radio, the Worldwide Web, and the Internet are all mass media tools that can be used to spread lies. The tragedy is that we have built such an aura of belief around media-produced information that we believe what we see on media, often without questioning it. Just because it's on the Internet or television does not make it true. The truth will make you free. Truth will not cause confusion in the body of Christ, for God is not the author of confusion.

Not only does God hate a lying tongue, but He also hates "feet that [are] swift in running to mischief, a false witness that speaketh lies, and he that soweth discord among brethren" (Proverbs 6:18, 19).

Some people proclaim themselves to be

conveyors of news with the noble motive of keeping people informed. Even with the knowledge that their "news" might not be true and that it will cause discord in the body of Christ, they can't wait to reveal confidential information about the church, or to dissimulate the latest ecclesiastical gossip. These people will face God in horrible judgment, for they have done what He hates. They will be burned in the eternal furnace of His judgment as "tare" hypocrites. To escape this they must immediately cease from their devious activities and seek God's forgiveness and cleansing.

While it is easy to identify the unbridled tongue as a sure sign of hypocrisy (James 1:26), there are other very subtle characteristics of "tare" hypocrisy that are not so easily recognized. The disturbing thing for the last-days church is that though they are often overlooked by shallow Christians, they are very numerous and prevalent in the body.

A carnal mind is a mark of a "tare" individual. Paul said, "For to be carnally minded is death; but to be spiritually minded is life and peace" (Romans 8:6). The phrase here "to be carnally minded" literally means to set affections on the things of the flesh. In verse 5 Paul had stated, "For they that are after the flesh do mind the things of the flesh." The term "do mind" is translated from the Greek word *phroneo*, which means to "set the heart on" or "set affections on." Paul says this kind of mind-set brings spiritual death. In verses 7 and 8 he further states that the carnal mind is at war with God and cannot please Him.

A major problem that can be attributed to "tare" people in the church is the terrible proliferation of carnal values that have replaced spiritual values. When leadership within the church is based on nepotism, political connections, the "buddy" system, and the power of money instead of on honest merit and godliness, then carnality is reigning. When members of the body seek the destruction and eradication of each other, when grudges and vengeance drive men to carnal acts, and when the lust for power and the leaving of a legacy rules their every action, then carnality has taken over and the fields are full of tares. When gossip and innuendo, maneuvering and posturing for political advantage, and unrepentance and unforgiveness are rampant, then like the lukewarm church of Laodicea, we are "wretched, and miserable, and poor, and blind, and naked" (Revelation 3:17). At this point magnificent sanctuaries, velvety soft pews, thunderous echoing choirs, and melodious strands of music no longer matter, for it is then that we have nauseated God—and God says, "I will spue thee out of my mouth" (v. 16).

Another point is worthy of our attention concerning these "tares." Notice Jesus identified them as "all things that offend" (Matthew 13:41). God has always displayed divine anger toward those who willingly and knowingly hurt members of the body of Christ. This is especially true when the hurt ones are young and tender "babes in Christ." Jesus said it best: "But whoso shall offend one of these little ones which believe in me, it were better for him that a millstone were hanged about his neck, and that he were drowned in the depth of the sea" (18:6). The millstone punishment refers to a method of execution used by the ancient Syrians, Greeks, and Egyptians, involving a stone 18 inches in diameter and 3 inches thick. This weight around the neck quickly sank the hapless victim to the bottom of the ocean, and the sudden rush of salt water into the lungs brought horrible death. Yet Jesus says the wrath of God on those who knowingly cause hurt, disenchantment, and disillusionment on tender Christians will be far worse than "millstone" execution. This lesson is for "tare" hypocrites whose influence in the body is admired and respected but the revelation of their sinful lifestyle brings harm, hurt, and backsliding to those whose confidence in them has been woefully misplaced. No wonder Jesus declared, "But woe to that man by whom the offence cometh!" (18:7).

Tares want to dominate the field and overshadow the true wheat. Tares attempt to climb skyward to get the most benefit of the sun and falling rain. Tares grow strong and tall for a time; but as sure as God reigns in heaven, the angelic scythe is coming that will cut the tare and it will be bundled with all tares and destroyed.

Jesus gave us this parable as a warning. The wise and prudent will seek God's discernment in these crucial last days to know the wheat from the tares. The wise husbandman will know and take heed.

Finally, one must view this parable from a last-days perspective. When Jesus made the statement "So shall it be in the end of this world" (Matthew 13:40), it became evident that His portrait of the wheat and tares was one of the church in the last days. The lesson is that in the last days carnality, hypocrisy, sin, and falsehood will plague the church even while revival grows and flourishes. Once again this parable illustrates the paradox of the last days. While God pours His Spirit out upon all flesh (Joel 2:28), there is an abounding of iniquity because love is "waxing" cold (Matthew 24:12). Tares among the wheat are awaiting the end-time harvest of judgment angels and the wrath of God. This is not a popular message, and those who despise it are many. But it is with this scripture that God would have us remember the parable of the wheat and tares: "Nevertheless the foundation of God standeth sure, having this seal, The Lord knoweth them that are his. And, Let every one that nameth the name of Christ depart from iniquity" (2 Timothy 2:19).

CHAPTER 7

Jesus on the Mount of Olives

And as he sat upon the mount of Olives, the disciples came unto him privately, saying, Tell us, when shall these things be? and what shall be the sign of thy coming, and of the end of the world? (Matthew 24:3).

The most commanding view of the Temple was obtained from the Mount of Olives. Here among the groves of olive trees and desert stones, one could look down upon the city of Jerusalem and immediately be struck with awe at the majesty of the Temple. Herod's temple, approximately 500 cubits square, was made of white marble. The stones, with which the Temple was constructed, were a marvel of human engineering. Josephus, the first-century Jewish historian, states that some of these stones were 94 feet long, 10 1/2 feet high, and 13 feet wide. There were 162 solid marble columns that held up the porches, which were 52 feet high. This Temple was truly one of the wonders of the ancient world.

As Jesus looked upon the Temple from the Mount of Olives, He uttered a remarkable prophecy concerning its destruction. He said to the disciples, "See ye not all these things? verily I say unto you, There shall not be left here one stone upon another, that shall not be thrown down" (Matthew 24:2).

This prophecy would come to fruition in A.D. 70. Titus, the Roman military genius, would besiege the city of Jerusalem and bring it crashing to the ground. The barbarous Roman military machine would butcher more than a million Jews. Most of the survivors would be scattered throughout the empire and sold as slaves. It was during this fall of the great city of Jerusalem, that Jesus' prophecy concerning the Temple came to pass. The Temple was torn down and every stone was removed. Teams of horses pulled plows over the ground where the Jews once worshiped the one true God. The prophecies of Jesus are always accurate to the letter.

That day on the Mount of Olives, the disciples heard this prophecy of the Temple stones and immediately were shaken. To an ancient Jew the Temple was the center of life. No true Jew would even walk in the streets of Jerusalem without the Temple being partially in his view. Its geographic location in the city permitted this and only added to the people's adoration of this worship edifice. Its magnificence and overwhelming presence made it seem invulnerable as its white marble glowed in the bright sun of the Middle East. For Jesus to tell these Galileans that their Temple would be destroyed meant only one thing to them: the end of the world must be coming. Not understanding the order of future events, their minds longed for further explanation from the Master. It is at this point that Jesus was asked the two questions of Matthew 24:3 that would lead to one of the most remarkable passages in the Bible concerning the conditions that will exist in the end of time.

In verses 4-6, Jesus addressed these disciples specifically. Some powerful, spiritual, historical, and political things would take place in their lifetime and yet those events would not signal the end of time.

Therefore Jesus warned them, "Take heed that no man deceive you" (v. 4).

This would be a great lesson for each of us to learn today. Deception is a crafty tool of the Enemy and one he doesn't hesitate to use. Subtle deception was very successful on Adam and Eve, and he has found it effective on their descendants as well.

Jesus then identified the deception that these disciples would be faced with in their own time: "For many shall come in my name, saying, I am Christ; and shall deceive many" (v. 5). This prophecy could have a twofold meaning. It is a historical fact that in the first century, many false "messiahs" arose throughout the Middle East, especially in the Judean province. The great Pharisee Gamaliel, a doctor of the law and a teacher of Saul of Tarsus, told of two of these false messiahs. In Acts 5:36, he referred to a man by the name of Theudas, "boasting himself to be somebody." Gamaliel said that Theudas had as many as 400 followers, but he was slain and all his followers "were scattered, and brought to nought." In verse 37 he mentioned a man by the name of Judas of Galilee and reminded his listeners that Judas and all of his followers perished. In Josephus' *Book of Antiquities*, Book number 18, chapter I, Josephus refers to this Judas and tells us he led a revolt against Roman taxation and was destroyed.

Gamaliel used these illustrations of false messiahs to defend the early Christian movement. Though he was not a Christian, he stated, "And now I say unto you, Refrain from these men, and let them alone: for if this counsel or this work be of men, it will come to nought; but if it be of God, ye cannot overthrow it; lest haply ye be found even to fight against God" (vv. 38, 39).

Another possible meaning for Matthew 24:5 might have to do with false teaching within the ranks of Christianity. The disciples would face conflict relentlessly. Men would come in Jesus' name, promising salvation and would deceive many. Things have not changed. In fact, our day has seen an aggressive proliferation of false teaching and deceptive teachers. The warning of the apostle Paul to the Galatian church has never been more applicable: "But though we, or an angel from heaven, preach any other gospel unto you than that which we have preached unto you, let him be accursed" (Galatians 1:8).

In Matthew 24:6, Jesus told those disciples something that every generation needs to be aware of: "And ye shall hear of wars and rumours of wars: see that ye be not troubled: for all these things must come to pass, but the end is not yet."

This is a statement of pure reality. Ever since Cain rose up and slew his brother, Abel, mankind has been driven to war with his fellowman by sinful emotions. History is replete with wars of strife and anger. Wars for land, wars for causes, wars for thrones, and wars of civil strife have afflicted this planet like a horrible unending virus, and at the root of each war lies the coiled serpent of Eden's Garden. Jesus is saying in verse 6 that every war and rumor of a war does not mean that the end is coming. Human nature tends to think of the end of the world when catastrophic events occur. Jesus knew the dangers of this type of thinking. It is in the horrific moments of impending disaster that false prophecies of the flesh and sensationalism have a tendency to take over. This is why Jesus warned in Matthew 24:6, "See that ye be not *troubled*." The reason Jesus warned them against falling into the trap of anxiety was "for all these things must come to pass." This is a part of the human experience on this earth as long as man is under the curse of sin.

It is in verses 7 and 8 that Jesus pinpoints the conditions that immediately precede the end of time. He calls these conditions "the beginning of sorrows." No one prophet is more explicit in warnings against "date setting" than Jesus himself. In verse 36 He said, "But of that day and hour knoweth no man, no, not the angels of heaven, but my Father only." In Mark 13:32 He declared, "But of that day and that hour knoweth no man, no, not the angels which are in heaven, neither the Son, but the Father." What a statement! Can we even begin to fathom this admission? Here, Christ states that there is a bit of knowledge that belongs only to the Father. Some theologians speculate that this knowledge was kept from Christ or was unknown to Him while He was in His earthly body. Regardless of our inability to understand all that Mark 13:32 encompasses, one thing is crystal clear from this passage—it is futile to try to set a date for Christ's return. Anyone who attempts to do so is an impostor, a false prophet, or a tragically ignorant person where the Scripture is concerned. Christ further reiterated this position in Acts 1:7, when He told His inquiring disciples, "It is not for you to know the times or the seasons, which the Father hath put in his own power." The year, the month, the week, the day, the hour, the minute, the second, and yes, even the millisecond of time in the vastness of eternity when God will send Christ back to this earth is in the mind of God the Father. No man can know that day or hour, nor is it Scripturally possible to obtain that sacred bit of knowledge.

Jesus, however, graphically tells us of conditions which will exist on the earth that are so unique and will occupy such a profound place in history that we will be aware the time is very, very, near. He describes such conditions in Matthew 24:7.

Nation against nation. He begins with the three-letter word *for*. In English it is often used as a function word to indicate time—"when it does happen" or "when it does come," which is the meaning here. Christ had just said that every war or rumor of a war didn't mean the end was upon them. But in verse 7, He begins with this powerful little word, *for*. The meaning here is that when the end really comes, or is upon us, it will not be the ordinary pattern of war that has plagued Adam's race since the dawn of time, but it will be a time of "nation . . . against nation, and kingdom against kingdom."

The 20th century must surely be hailed as the most unique in the annals of mankind. Before it surfaced on the calendar of time, much of life on earth had remained unchanged for thousands of years. The technology and advancement in science and transportation were discussed at length in chapter 2—"Prophets and Pinpoints"—but all of this scientific advancement made the fulfillment of Matthew 24:7 a reality. Now the end would begin.

114

World War I rose up like a heinous monster and clasped its wicked talons around the throat of humanity. This was no small conflict. Historians refer to it as a time when the lights went out in Europe. It was known as "the Great War" and "the War to end all wars." Twenty-eight nations declared war against each other. Nearly 10 million soldiers died as a result of that war. Some 21 million soldiers were wounded on the battlefield. This war cost the fighting nations $337 billion. By 1918 it was costing $10 million an hour to fight this war. This war saw the emergence of airplanes, submarines, machine guns, tanks, poison gas, and hand grenades. The stench and horror of the trenches wafted across the air of Europe, and the smell of death filled the continent. At no time in all of human history had anyone seen anything like this. Napoleon's charges, Caesar's legions, and Nebuchadnezzar's armies paled in comparison with this kind of war. When it finally ended in the early morning hours of November 11, 1918, and fighting officially ceased on the Western Front at 11 a.m. the same day, the world shuddered as it breathed the air of peace once more. A League of Nations was formed and men declared that war was no more.

On September 1, 1939, just 21 years after World War I ended, World War II began. As bad as World War I was, World War II would be much, much worse. This time 59 nations would declare war against each other. This war would encircle the globe with killing and genocide on a scale never seen before by the human race. Historians agree that we will probably never know the total death toll of this war, but at least 17 million military deaths can be accounted for. The civilian death toll far eclipses that, for people died by the millions from starvation, bombing raids, massacres, death camps, epidemics, and other war-related causes. Killing took place in jungles, deserts, arid plains, rich-agricultural belts, cities, forests, oceans, and on the surface of rivers. The skies rained death from high-altitude bombers, and fighting planes drenched the clouds themselves with blood and metal shards. Adolph Hitler, Emperor Hirohito, Joseph Stalin, Winston Churchill, and Franklin Roosevelt became household names. Weaponry advanced far beyond what anyone could ever imagine was possible. High-altitude bombers engulfed cities in firestorms that melted steel beams deep into the ground. Aircraft carriers and submarines made the ocean a watery grave for hundreds of thousands of airmen and sailors.

On August 6, 1945, an American B-29 bomber dubbed the *Enola Gay* left the tiny island of Tinian in the South Pacific and dropped the atomic bomb on Hiroshima, Japan. It instantly incinerated over 100,000 people. Casualty totals would rise as high as 169,000 in the weeks that followed. Five square miles were vaporized in a moment of time. On August 9, just three days later, a second bomb would explode over Nagasaki. This time 40,000 people would instantly perish. The world would never be the same again. Man had now devised a weapon powerful enough to erase himself from the planet.

Since the time of World War I and World War II, there has been a constant pattern of "nation against nation, and kingdom against kingdom," the prophecy that Jesus said would signal the "beginning of sorrows." Our world has seen war on the Korean Peninsula, war throughout the Middle East, war in Southeast Asia, and war in almost every nation of Africa. There has been war between India and Pakistan, war in the Persian Gulf, war in Northern Ireland, war in the Balkans, war in Eastern Europe, and war among the nations of the old Soviet Socialist Republic. War has arisen between Britain and Argentina in the Falklands, and war between kingdoms and tribes in many Third World countries. No century in all of human history can match this in intensity. The death toll of 20th-century wars far exceeds anything that's ever happened. Listen to the Great Teacher! His lesson is poignant and plain! The beginning of sorrows, the end of the world, the end of the age—all of these are one and the same. They will be pinpointed by a different kind of war scenario. "Nation against nation" is the sign. We have seen it come to pass.

The tendency to wage international war was not the only prophecy, however, that Jesus gave. This powerful verse of Matthew 24:7 lists three other phenomena that would occur. Though each of the signs in this passage have occurred throughout human history, this prophecy would make no sense except for the fact that each of these things must occur on such a grand scale that they will be observed easily as being unique and unusual.

Famines. Notice here that the occurrence is identified in the plural. There are certain things that cause famine that these last days have produced with increasing frequency. The first is overpopulation. Statisticians tell us that over one-half of everybody who has ever been alive is alive right now on Planet Earth. The 1990 census estimated world population was 5,288,000,000. With a growth rate of 1.7

percent a year, this means earth's population will double every 41 years. On earth's largest continent of Asia there are 187 people living on every square mile. While world population has more than doubled since 1950, food supplies have more than tripled. Some agricultural scientists believe that if technology in food production continues to increase, it would be possible to grow enough food to feed the exploding population. So the question arises, How can there be a prediction of famine? The answer is simple really, and unrealistic optimism about the future should not cloud the reality of the recent past or the rapidly descending future. The truth is that the 20th century has seen the worst famines in history. In 1943 in Bengal of eastern India, 1 1/2 million people died of starvation. In 1917 in Russia during the Bolshevik Revolution, untold millions succumbed to starvation, and even cannibalism became frequent. Scientists estimate that since the 1960s, millions have died of famine in the region of Africa known as the Sahel, just south of the Sahara desert. Along the Huang He River in northern China, in an area known as "China's Sorrow," between 1929 and 1930 over 2 million people died of starvation. Over a million died of starvation in the tiny nation of Biafra between 1967 and 1970.

119

Many areas plagued by modern famine are far removed from industrialized society and ready food supplies. Weather conditions like droughts, floods, typhoons, and hail negate any positive effects like advanced technology. Wars and political upheaval often leave homeless refugees to suffer and die from starvation.

Jesus said marked famine would be a sign of the end of time, and history has proven Him to be correct. The population of earth continues to explode, and the elements of nature that control food production remain out of mankind's control. A higher power is the Architect of history and His predictions never fail.

Pestilences. Jesus then went on to say that pestilence, or disease, would be a signal sign of the last days. Again one wonders how this can be so. Life expectancy on earth has risen from 46.5 years in 1950 to 64 years today. Medical science stands as a monument to man's ingenuity with laser surgery, miracle drugs, and diagnostic techniques that defy the human imagination. Yet Jesus, who never errs in His prophecies, says there will be a time of pestilence. And despite the advances of science and the dreamers of utopia smiling their radiant best, the pestilence prophecy is in full fruition. And why shouldn't it be? We fill the diet of animals we eat with growth hormones and steroid drugs. We process our food with a myriad of chemicals and preservatives. Our air is full of poisons, and our streams and rivers are full of chemicals and pollutants. Biologists warn us not to eat fish from our rivers due to mercury and toxin levels. Carcinogens, or cancer-causing agents, abound in everything from cosmetics to upholstery. The sexual mores of our society have produced a floodtide of diseases like AIDS, herpes, syphilis, gonorrhea, and hepatitis. The stress of modern times fills cardiac units, produces strokes, and keeps the psychiatrists busy. In underdeveloped countries, war and famine have produced cholera epidemics and plagues of many varieties. Viruses like E-coli defy the medical world, and new superstrains of germs have arisen that are impervious to antibiotic treatment.

Disease has always been with man. When Adam and Eve left the Garden in their sin, they were destined to die. Sin brought death. This age, however, has brought about a growth of disease that this planet has never faced. We tremble at the thought of despots and dictators who may use disease and plagues in their weapons of mass destruction, for we know that against such an attack the entire world is very vulnerable. Perhaps that will be next and further fulfill this word of prophecy in Matthew 24:7.

Earthquakes. Finally, Jesus indicates that a sign will come from the earth itself—"and earthquakes, in divers places" (Matthew 24:7). An earthquake is a powerful force. The energy released by a large earthquake may be equal to 180 metric tons of TNT. It can release an energy level 10,000 times greater than the first atomic bomb. Earthquakes are caused when the plates of the earth's surface rupture and shift. These ruptures, or faults, lie beneath the earth's surface. Some, like the San Andreas fault in California, are visible.

Though earthquakes have occurred throughout history, they were actually not that frequent until the latter part of the 19th century and throughout the 20th century. Today, seismologists estimate that as many as a million earthquakes a year occur, most of them beneath the surface of the sea.

In the light of Jesus' prophecy, it's very intriguing to learn that since 1905 there have been at least 29 earthquakes that have registered above 8.0 on the Richter scale. At least three of these quakes registered above 9 on the Richter scale. Many of the great cities of the United States stand in great risk of a devastating earthquake in the near future, for they sit in close proximity to extremely unstable fault systems. San Francisco, Los Angeles, St. Louis, Memphis, Charleston (South Carolina), and Portland (Oregon) are American cities where earthquakes have occurred and could occur again.

The Book of Revelation speaks of a time during the Great Tribulation when a great earthquake literally shakes the entire earth. When the sixth seal is opened, John said a great earthquake occurred (6:12). In verse 14, he said the effect of its power was so great that "every mountain and island were moved out of their places." Imagine such power! But men should remember that the God who spoke the universe into existence has just such power and He can use it at His discretion.

The severity and increase in the frequency of earthquakes remind us of another scripture that came from the pen of the apostle Paul. In Romans 8:22 he declared, "For we know that the whole creation goaneth and travaileth in pain together until now." The earth has been racked and infested by sin for at least six millenniums, and the wretchedness of it all has all of creation groaning in travail. The earth itself shakes with anger and consternation, awaiting the redemption of the creation. This redemption will one day come. Every time this earth quakes, we, who believe in the prophecy that the Great Teacher gave to that little group of Galileans on the Mount of Olives, should rejoice and be glad that "redemption draweth nigh"(Luke 21:28). The time is at hand. The Teacher has taught His lesson.

CHAPTER 8

Jesus and the Wedding Garment

And when the king came in to see the guests, he saw there a man which had not on a wedding garment: And he saith unto him, Friend, how camest thou in hither not having a wedding garment? And he was speechless (Matthew 22:11, 12).

Parables are stories that take common occurrences and true-to-life customs and use them to illustrate profound spiritual lessons. Jesus was the master of the parable as He was with everything. The parable of the wedding feast in Matthew 22 was the third parable that Jesus taught to the Jews in the

Temple concerning the Kingdom. The first was the parable of the two sons who were commanded by their father to go and work in his vineyard (Matthew 21:28-32). The first son said no, but later repented and went. The second son said yes, but never went. Jesus used this to illustrate that the repentant, though harlots and sinners, would go into the Kingdom before unrepentant, self-righteous Pharisees.

The second parable given by the Great Teacher in the Temple was that of the vineyard and the wicked husbandmen (21:33-41). The parable tells of a householder who plants a vineyard, builds a tower, and leases it to husbandmen, or vinedressers. When it is time to collect his due reward, the servants of the householder are slain one after another. The great man finally sends his son, but the wicked husbandmen slay him also and attempt to seize the property for themselves. The great man then destroys those wicked murderers and gives the vineyard to more worthy men. Here is an illustration to Israel, which rejected the message of the prophets and apostles and finally rejected the Son of God himself. They would suffer horribly and the message of the true vine would go to the Gentiles.

But it is in this third parable given in the

126

Temple (Matthew 22) that we see a powerful last-days truth of a prophetical nature. This is the parable of the wedding and the wedding garment:

> And Jesus answered and spake unto them again by parables, and said, The kingdom of heaven is like unto a certain king, which made a marriage for his son, and sent forth his servants to call them that were bidden to the wedding: and they would not come. Again, he sent forth other servants, saying, Tell them which are bidden, Behold, I have prepared my dinner: my oxen and my fatlings are killed, and all things are ready: come unto the marriage. But they made light of it, and went their ways, one to his farm, another to his merchandise: And the remnant took his servants, and entreated them spitefully, and slew them. But when the king heard thereof, he was wroth: and he sent forth his armies, and destroyed those murderers, and burned up their city. Then saith he to his servants, The wedding is ready, but they which were bidden were not worthy. Go ye therefore into the highways, and as many as ye shall find, bid to the marriage. So those servants went out into the highways, and gathered

together all as many as they found, both bad and good: and the wedding was furnished with guests. And when the king came in to see the guests, he saw there a man which had not on a wedding garment: And he saith unto him, Friend, how camest thou in hither not having a wedding garment? And he was speechless. Then said the king to the servants, Bind him hand and foot, and take him away, and cast him into outer darkness; there shall be weeping and gnashing of teeth. For many are called, but few are chosen (Matthew 22:1-14).

The parable begins when Jesus likens the kingdom of heaven unto a certain king who plans a marriage for his son. He sends forth servants to invite selected guests to come to the wedding (v. 3). Upon the refusal of these guests to attend, another guest list is given to another group of servants, and their invitation is given with a description of the fine feast and immaculate provisions that await them when they arrive at the wedding (v. 4). It's interesting to note that these invited guests make light of the invitation and indicate they have more important matters to attend to, such as their farms and businesses (v. 5). Out of these invited guests, those who do not return

to their everyday obligations torture and slay the
king's servants who brought the invitation (v. 6).
The king's anger is kindled white-hot and he sends
armies to slay these wicked men and burn up their
cities (v. 7). Verse 8 is an indictment of the guests
who rejected the invitation. The king simply states,
"They which were bidden were not worthy." Verses 9
and 10 tell how the king decided to invite anyone
willing to come, and soon the wedding was furnished
with guests.

The first part of this parable must be considered prophetically before the rest of the story, which
will leave us with a profound significance. The relationship of Christ and the church is often symboli-
cally portrayed as a marriage union. In Ephesians
5:25, Paul said, "Husbands, love your wives, even as
Christ also loved the church, and gave himself for
it." In Revelation 21:9, John is given an invitation
by one of the seven angels, saying, "Come hither, I
will shew thee the bride, the Lamb's wife."

This relationship of Christ and the church is
one of beauty, fidelity, and holiness. Through this
parable we see how God has dealt with humanity to
woo them to become a part of His glorious kingdom
through the redemption offered by His Son, Jesus
Christ.

Like the nation of Israel, the intended guests rejected the invitation and killed those who delivered it. Israel had rejected the prophets and stoned her messengers of salvation. When Jesus looked out over the city of Jerusalem in the waning hours prior to His death, He was overcome with grief. He wept as He cried out, "O Jerusalem, Jerusalem, thou that killest the prophets, and stonest them which are sent unto thee, how often would I have gathered thy children together, even as a hen gathereth her chickens under her wings, and ye would not! Behold, your house is left unto you desolate" (Matthew 23:37, 38).

A modern last-days analogy can be gained from the story of the parable in Matthew 22, especially concerning the guests who rejected the invitation. Notice in verse 5, we find guests whose everyday lifestyles and responsibilities mean more than the opportunity to be a part of the wedding of the king's son. Like the men of Noah's day and the people of Sodom and Gomorrah on the eve of their own destruction, their concern with building, buying, planting, and selling consumed them. The lesson here is the danger of living as if this world were the only world we'll ever have to live in. This is why the apostle John so emphatically stated, "Love not the world, neither the things that are in the world. If any

130

man love the world, the love of the Father is not in him" (I John 1:15).

There is no compatibility between the love of the world and the love of the Father. The age-old conflict of serving two masters is the point in question. Jesus said it best: "No servant can serve two masters: for either he will hate the one, and love the other; or else he will hold to the one, and despise the other. Ye cannot serve God and mammon" (Luke 16:13). Has this generation fallen in love with this world? The evidence would seem to indicate it has. Like a busy colony of ants, we are in constant motion to live, work, develop, improve, and embellish our world. Men do everything in their power to live longer and to enjoy this earth to the fullest, with no thought given to the longer, never-ending life span of eternity. The Bible is a book given to us by God himself. It teaches us how to live in this world as in preparation for the much-longer and more important realm of eternity. A loss of the sense of eternity means men lose values like morality, kindness, spiritual fervor, and devotion to God. This is the crux of modern society's spiritual collapse. Like those who rejected the wedding invitation, who had rather farm or sell than to celebrate with the king, there is living now a generation that had rather invest in this world. Twenty years after their death, they will be only a faded memory in the minds of a few who knew them, and eternity for them will be just beginning.

Finally, the first part of this parable reminds us of two things. First, the king opened up his wedding invitation to all, so God invites all to participate in redemption. "And the Spirit and the bride say, Come. And let him that heareth say, Come. And let him that is athirst come. And whosoever will, let him take the water of life freely" (Revelation 22:17). No one is left out or ostracized from this invitation. The wedding will be furnished with guests. Second, these guests are socially and culturally diverse. Matthew 22:10 says they found "both bad and good." The meaning here has to do with social desirability. Vagabonds and the elite, rich and poor, royalty and paupers, skilled and ignorant, and men and women of every culture, race, and nationality will make up the guest list. God has no prejudice. Redemption is for all. Every nation, tribe, and kingdom will have representatives at the wedding. And the guests will be glad they came.

The final part of this great parable has to do with a confrontation that takes place between a guest and the king. This confrontation should grip the heart of every reader with a conviction of examination.

Among the unique customs of the ancient Middle East was one concerning a wedding garment. It was customary for every rich host, especially royalty, to provide all their wedding guests with a special garment. Such was the case in this parable. It is especially important in this parable because among these guests were beggars, street people, and vagabonds from the highways and byways. Their rags and plain attire would have been out of place in the royal setting of the palace wedding. However, the beauty of the kingly garment would equalize standing among all the guests.

So it is in Christ. Regardless of our background and earthly status, we have been robed according to the will of the King. We wear the garment of salvation. Psalm 149:4 declares, "The Lord . . . will beautify the meek with salvation." This way there is no status or class—no "big *I* and little *you*." All are the same in Christ. No wonder the apostle James was so adamant in his rebuke of those who had "respect of persons." He condemned those in the church that honored the rich or renowned but showed disdain for the poor and indigent. He said, "But if ye have respect to persons, ye commit sin, and are convinced of the law as transgressors" (James 2:9). One of the sins of the last-days church that finds us wanting is when we boast about our "good class of people," or our "money crowd." All of the redeemed are a good class of people. Money means nothing to a God who paves streets with pure gold. This parable teaches that the king wanted to clothe all of his guests the same way.

Matthew 22:11-14 tells of the confrontation that took place. The king enters the hall and finds a man who does not have on a wedding garment. The king wants to know how he got in without the right garment.

At these ancient weddings, the garments were given to the guests prior to the event and were a clear mark of identification. Evidently, this man's garment was so much like the real thing that nobody could tell the difference—nobody, that is, but the king. The king's piercing eyes knew immediately that the man's garment was not the real thing. The king always knows the real from the counterfeit. No master counterfeiter or illusionist can fool the eyes of the king. In ancient times no greater insult could be given a host than to refuse to wear the given wedding garment. When the king confronted this man, the Bible says he was speechless. He was bound and cast into outer darkness for this insult to the king.

Could the lesson be any more plain? What a

truth God is trying to tell us! The king is on the way to examine the invited guest. Only *His* garment is acceptable. Any attempt to deceive God by "garments" of good works or religious hypocrisy is futile. The King will know and see what we are wearing.

Another thing that is striking in this scene is the fact that this man fit in perfectly until the king examined the crowd. A real danger in the last-days church world is the pretense of Christianity practiced by so many. People can have all the moves down perfectly. They can know the nomenclature of the Christian faith and do all the religious things required of them. They can even play church, sing, worship, and do good works. They will fit in just like the guest with the unacceptable garment. No one will know his or her true life. Perhaps this is the reason for so many "double lives" being practiced. Many people in the modern era have a church life and a secular or worldly life. Their behavior and practices at home, on the job, in the car, and on vacation differ substantially from what they claim and project in church. In church they "amen" the sterner points of the preacher's message and wave their arms in worship and adoration while they lift melodious voices of praise to God. Once outside the sanctuary, however, a noticeably unrighteous attitude is manifested in their personality. What they watch on television, the music they listen to, their dealings in the business world, and their relationships with family, friends, and neighbors seldom reflect a heart that has been transformed by the redeeming power of Christ's blood. They are not wearing a wedding garment. The one they wear gets them accepted in church and a nice eulogy will be performed at their funeral, but the King knows the truth.

One day the Rapture trumpet will sound, and in a millisecond of time the King of kings will review all wedding guests and will instantly ascertain who has on the right garments. Those who do will rise to meet Him in the air for the royal wedding celebration. Those not adorned in His garment will soon realize the horror of their predicament. The game will be over and the truth will come out.

We are nearing that hour. Soon the King will announce as He did in Matthew 22:4, "All things are ready: come unto the marriage."

CHAPTER 9

The Rapture and Celebration

For the Lord himself shall descend from heaven with a shout, with the voice of the archangel, and with the trump of God: and the dead in Christ shall rise first: Then we which are alive and remain shall be caught up together with them in the clouds, to meet the Lord in the air: and so shall we ever be with the Lord. Wherefore comfort one another with these words (I Thessalonians 4:16-18).

For our conversation [citizenship] is in heaven; from whence also we look for the Saviour, the Lord Jesus Christ: who shall change our vile body, that it may be fashioned like unto his glorious body, according to the working whereby he is able even to subdue all things unto himself (Philippians 3:20, 21).

For yet a little while, and he that shall come will come, and will not tarry (Hebrews 10:37).

And if I [Jesus Christ] go and prepare a place for you, I will come again, and receive you unto myself; that where I am, there ye may be also (John 14:3).

All study of last-days theology leads to one primary event—the Rapture, or the catching away of the church to meet Christ in the air. Although the word *rapture* is not found in the Bible, the concept is presented vividly. Christ will return in midair; the saints will be glorified, and caught up to Him in an instant of time. This glorified church will then be carried into the presence of God for a celebration of the eternal union of Christ and His bride. This is a concept found repeatedly in Scripture.

Literally thousands of volumes have been penned through the ages, dealing with signs of Christ's return. Some individuals have spent the majority of their lives searching for and writing about the date of Christ's return. Many study geopolitical events and historical occurrences surrounding the nation of

Israel, and then correlate them in relation to their prophetic importance concerning Christ's return.

Much less however, has been written or spoken about the actual event itself. What will it be like? What things will occur at the time of the Rapture that will profoundly affect this planet? The rapture of the church will undoubtedly become a catalyst for earthshaking events, but what will they be? How will the world respond? How will shocked and terrified "church people" react when the realization that the Rapture has taken place dawns on them? How soon after this event will the Tribulation begin to unfold? For those who are caught up to meet Christ, what can they expect as eternity unfolds for them? Since we are changed into a glorified body, exactly what will our knowledge level be like? Will we know each other?

As you can see, the Biblical event of the Rapture unleashes many intense questions. The good news is that the Bible answers most of them. Those left unanswered are left unanswered for a reason. Some things are reserved for the mind of God and it is important to understand that.

Let us now consider the event itself. What does the Bible have to say about the Rapture? What are the characteristics of this event? What can the world expect?

At this point, a definition is probably in order. When we use the word *rapture,* we are referring to the sudden, unannounced descent of Christ in the air above the earth. At this time, according to Paul, the dead in Christ will first be resurrected, followed immediately by the glorification of both the living and the resurrected saints. Then together, they will all rise to meet Christ in the air (1 Thessalonians 4:16-18). Then, according to Revelation 19:6-9, a marriage celebration will take place in heaven. This will be a celebration of the eternal union of Christ and those who have joined Him in the first resurrection as redeemed and glorified saints of God. While this is taking place, there will be great and horrible tribulation on earth as the wrath of God is poured out without measure, according to Jesus in Matthew 24:21.

This catching away of both the dead and living saints, as Christ stands in midair, is not to be confused with the event that takes place at the end of the Tribulation when Christ returns to stand upon the earth (Revelation 19:11-16). Here, the returning Christ is seen riding upon a white horse, clothed in a robe dipped in blood, and on the robe and on His thigh is a name written: "KING OF KINGS, AND LORD OF LORDS" (v. 16). In this passage the armies of heaven are following Him, also riding upon white horses and "clothed in fine linen, white and clean" (v. 14). According to verse 8, the "fine linen" identifies this army as the righteous saints. They are returning to earth to rule and reign with Christ as kings and priests during His millennial reign of peace (20:6). This period of time will be dealt with later and is only mentioned here to identify it as being distinctly different from the Rapture. Jesus was referring to the Rapture when He said, "I will come again, and receive you unto myself" (John 14:3). It is the same Rapture that Paul refers to in I Corinthians 15:51, 52 when he so emphatically declared:

> Behold, I shew you a mystery; We shall not all sleep, but we shall all be changed, in a moment, in the twinkling of an eye, at the last trump: for the trumpet shall sound, and the dead shall be raised incorruptible, and we shall be changed.

There are some characteristics of this event that are of particular importance which we need to take note of. More than that, these characteristics are in themselves both shocking and sobering food for thought.

First of all, the Rapture will be without warning. This is particularly interesting to our modern age. We live in a world unique in the annals of history. World-wide, simultaneous telecommunications are a fact of life in this age. The entire world sees the newsworthy events around the globe while they are taking place, and most of these events are predicted and preannounced. Due to the world's being under constant space-satellite surveillance, no military maneuvers or global movement takes place without the notice of military observers. Worldwide news networks from around the globe accurately predict trends, predicated on intricate knowledge that exists between nations and their various braintrusts. Even cataclysmic natural disasters, with the exception of earthquakes, are forecast with amazing accuracy. Hurricanes and typhoons no longer catch nations unawares. Seismic scientists now understand the geological conditions that exist prior to volcanic eruption; and though earthquakes themselves remain relatively unpredictable, the stability of fault-lines that precede earthquakes can be measured and trends for the future can be established somewhat. The bottom line is that most momentous events on this earth—whether they are political, military, or natural—can be forecast with a relative degree of accuracy.

With this knowledge firmly in place, you can readily see that the Rapture will be a shocking event. The Scripture is very clear—there will be no advance warning of this event. Jesus was very plain on the subject of the surprise nature of the Rapture. Listen to the voice of the Master:

> But of that day and hour knoweth no man, no, not the angels of heaven, but my Father only (Matthew 24:36).

> Watch therefore: for ye know not what hour your Lord doth come (Matthew 24:42).

> Therefore be ye also ready: for in such an hour as ye think not the Son of man cometh (Matthew 24:44).

> But of that day and that hour knoweth no man, no, not the angels which are in heaven, neither the Son, but the Father. Take ye heed, watch and pray: for ye know not when the time is (Mark 13:32, 33).

> For as a snare shall it come on all them that dwell on the face of the whole earth (Luke 21:35).

It is clear from these passages that Christ has issued a warning to Christians of all ages about the mystery of the Rapture. No man will ever be able to ascertain the time of the coming of the Lord. There will be no prior announcement, no first alert—it will just happen. The Father will declare that the time has arrived, the angelic trumpet will sound, and Christ will descend with the triumphant shout of the Bridegroom. The dead in Christ and those living saints who lead redeemed and holy lives will rise to meet Him in the air. With these thoughts in mind—that this event will be totally unannounced and that our only warnings will be those characteristics of the age given in Scripture—we are faced with a number of implications. Therefore, we must conclude that preparation is to be constant. We must be ready at all times. Things in our lives that would separate us from God must be constantly eradicated. Those who are Rapture-conscious cannot allow works of the flesh such as grudges, lingering hatred, jealousy, strife, wrath, bitterness, smoldering anger, hidden sinful lifestyles, and unforgiveness to remain in their lives. Every believer must practice I John 2:1, 2, in spirit and in deed. Here the apostle of love says, "My little children, these things write I unto you, that ye sin not. And if any man sin, we have an advocate with the

Father, Jesus Christ the righteous: And he is the pro-
pitiation for our sins: and not for our's only, but
also for the sins of the whole world."

The believer must, through repentance and faith
in Christ, accept Christ's provision of blood for any
and all sin he has allowed in his life. That sin must
then be forsaken forever. This is what Paul meant
when he said in Romans 6:1, 2, "What shall we say
then? Shall we continue in sin, that grace may
abound? God forbid. How shall we that are dead to
sin, live any longer therein?" Sin is not to rule us
any longer. In verse 14, Paul says, "sin shall not have
dominion over you."

Yet all of us have struggled with the attack of
the Enemy and his relentless war on the saints. Our
spirits are willing, but our flesh is weak. There is
only one solution for this inner struggle against sin
and temptation. Jesus said to the sleepy disciples in
Gethsemane's shadows, "Watch and pray, that ye en-
ter not into temptation: the spirit indeed is willing,
but the flesh is weak" (Matthew 26:41).

Paul tells us how we must walk in the Spirit
to be free from condemnation. In Romans 8:1, he
says, "There is therefore now no condemnation to
them which are in Christ Jesus, who walk not after
the flesh, but after the Spirit." He further states,

145

"For to be carnally minded is death; but to be spiritually minded is life and peace" (v. 6). To be Rapture-ready we must be people who are free from the condemnation of sin. To have this freedom according to Romans 8:1, we must "walk . . . after the Spirit." The simple fact of Scripture is that "no servant can serve two masters" (Luke 16:13). Therefore the conclusion is easy to draw. Since the Rapture will be unannounced and sudden, those who are alive and wish to go must be ready at that moment. There will be no time for repentance or for restitution . . . no time for forgiveness or for prayer . . . no time to give what is owed . . . no time for impassioned pleas . . . no time for preparation. It will happen, and it will be over. In less time than it will take you to read this sentence, the Rapture will take place.

Second, the return of Christ will be a swift return. It will literally happen very fast. Since our world is velocity-conscious, the question naturally arises, How fast?

In I Corinthians 15:52, Paul says the event will take place *"in a moment,* in the twinkling of an eye." The Greek terminology here is the phrase *en atomos.* This means "in an atom of time." Atoms of course, are the smallest components of the elements;

146

they are the minute building blocks of the universe. It is the phrase "an atom of time" that is used to describe the swiftness of the Rapture. Swifter than the blinking or winking of an eyelid, the Lord will descend. The twinkling of the eye is an apt description. This occurs when the eyeball itself is covered with a thin liquid film and literally shines, or is said to "twinkle." Heightened emotions like joy or great sadness frequently bring a glisten to the eye that lasts only a millisecond of time. What a comparison! The Rapture will bring both great joy and overwhelming sadness.

The joy that will fill the heart of a believer when Christ comes is beyond description. Paul quoted the prophet Isaiah (64:4) when he declared the glory of this wonder in I Corinthians 2:9: "But as it is written, Eye hath not seen, nor ear heard, neither have entered into the heart of man, the things which God hath prepared for them that love him." The swiftness of the Rapture will bring great and indescribable joy to the waiting saints. And yet, just as quickly there will be overwhelming sadness to be dealt with by those who remain behind.

One can only imagine the horror of a time when family members have suddenly disappeared. An empty place in a bed, a coworker who can't be found, a parent looking for a child, a frantic search for a missing companion—this will be a time of global mystery and confusion on a scale the world has never seen.

If Christians who are ready are operating automobiles, planes, trucks, tractors, or oxcarts, those mobile devices will suddenly be left without operators. There will be computers without fingers on the keyboard and important transactions left in limbo. There will be hot stoves unattended, water left running, dogs with no hand on their leash, a turning lathe and a dropped chisel, textbooks and pencils sliding off desks, unwatched televisions, and empty chairs at half-empty plates left at the table.

Terror will begin to unfold when those who are left behind realize just what has really happened. Those who had an earthly connection with these raptured saints through kinship or friendship will probably understand right away what has taken place. If they are smart enough and are able to regain their composure, they will begin to search the Scriptures and the writings of those with prophetical understanding for a solution to their dilemma and horror. Their search of the Scriptures will reveal to them an earth headed for disaster. Events will swiftly begin to take place and every aspect of life on this planet will be affected. These details await us in a later chapter, but suffice it to say that within hours after the Rapture, those who understand their situations will be wise to resign themselves to the reality of what has happened and begin to call upon God for their own salvation (Acts 2:21).

Finally, the Rapture will be a return of great power. Power is what is needed to complete the glorification of the body. Paul had a number of things to say about the transformation of our bodies, from the corruptible and mortal to the incorruptible and immortal. In Philippians 3:20, 21, he states, "For our conversation [citizenship] is in heaven; from whence also we look for the Saviour, the Lord Jesus Christ: who shall change our vile body, that it may be fashioned like unto his glorious body, according to the working whereby he is able even to subdue all things unto himself." In 1 Corinthians 15:51-54, he makes one of the grandest pronouncements in all of Scripture:

> Behold, I shew you a mystery; We shall not all sleep, but we shall be changed, in a moment, in the twinkling of an eye, at the last trump: for the trumpet shall sound, and the dead shall be raised incorruptible, and we shall be changed. For this corruptible must

149

put on incorruption, and this mortal must
put on immortality. So when this corruptible shall have put on incorruption, and this
mortal shall have put on immortality, then
shall be brought to pass the saying that is
written, Death is swallowed up in victory.

It will take the power of God's hand for this
change to take place, and again it is the apostle Paul
who tells us exactly how this will transpire: "But if
the Spirit of him that raised up Jesus from the dead
dwell in you, he that raised up Christ from the dead
shall also quicken your mortal bodies by his Spirit
that dwelleth in you"(Romans 8:11). It will be the
same power of the Holy Spirit that raised Christ
from the dead that will quicken the bodies of the
saints at the Rapture. Imagine, if you will, a sudden
burst of power flowing through you, unannounced,
unexpected, and accompanied by angelic trumpeters
as instantly you are changed and propelled into the
presence of God.

Paul, in Philippians 3:21, said that our glorified bodies will be "fashioned like unto his glorious body," speaking of Christ. We know that after
His resurrection, Christ appeared and disappeared at
will. He talked and could be seen. We know that

according to Luke 24:30, and verses 42, 43, He "sat at meat" with His disciples both at Emmaus and at Jerusalem. In the latter incident He ate broiled fish and a piece of honeycomb. We also know that after His resurrection, Jesus prepared a meal for the disciples beside the Sea of Galilee (see John 21:12, 13). We may expect our glorified bodies to be capable of the same things.

Though we may not understand all the intricacies involved in the nature of a glorified body, we do know it is a spiritual body that can never die or suffer any punishment. Revelation 20:6 declares, "Blessed and holy is he that hath part in the first resurrection: on such the second death hath no power, but they shall be priests of God and of Christ, and shall reign with him a thousand years."

The Bible gives us brief glimpses into what will occur for these raptured saints in the presence of God. In 1 Thessalonians 4:17, Paul says that they will remain with God forever. Never again will they be where they cannot be in the presence of Christ. The promise here is one of finality. "And so shall we ever be with the Lord" is a statement that leaves no room for debate.

We know that the celebration that goes on for the period of time that the earth is in tribulation is one referred to as a banquet or celebration supper. Revelation 19:9 refers to it as "the marriage supper of the Lamb." We also know from verse 8, that God grants that these raptured saints be clothed "in fine linen, clean and white." The fine linen represents their righteousness made possible by the blood of the Lamb.

Paul talked of crowns that will be given to the saints in heaven. In 2 Timothy 4:8, he mentioned a "crown of righteousness" that would be given to him and also "unto all them . . . that love his appearing," meaning the raptured saints. In 1 Thessalonians 2:19 he spoke of a "crown of rejoicing" that would be ours "in the presence of our Lord Jesus Christ at his coming." James promised for the believer a "crown of life, which the Lord hath promised" for "the man that endureth temptation" (James 1:12). The apostle Peter said, "And when the chief Shepherd shall appear, ye shall receive a crown of glory that fadeth not away" (1 Peter 5:4). It is easy to see from these scriptures that in addition to fine wedding garments, crowns will be given to the raptured saints at the celebration of Christ's marriage to the church.

It is concerning these crowns, however, that one of the most significant events of all takes place during this celebration. In Revelation 4:10, we find

24 elders before the throne of God, casting their crowns at His feet and worshiping Him who lives forever and ever. How could any of us feel worthy to wear a crown in the presence of the King of kings and the Lord of lords? Every brief glimpse into the throne room of God given us in Scripture finds the creatures of heaven and earth falling prostrate before Him. Moses, after seeing the hinder parts of God, had to place a veil over his face, after he came down from Mount Sinai for it glowed with God's glory (see Exodus 33:18-23; 34:29-35). When Gideon saw an angel of God, he thought he was going to die (Judges 6:22, 23). Isaiah declared "Woe is me! for I am undone," after he had seen the Lord "high and lifted up" (6:1, 5). John, on the rocky isle of Patmos, fell as a dead man when he saw Christ standing in the midst of the seven golden candlesticks (Revelation 1:17).

The truth is that when we see the One of whom we have sung about, preached about, prayed to, and worshiped, we will be overwhelmed with adoration and praise. The journey that we began as new-born babes, infected with the seed of sin innate in Adam's race, will finally be over. Somewhere in the course of that human journey, we will have accepted

God's redeemer, Jesus Christ, and we will have been forgiven of our sinful estate. Then, we'll stand eternally redeemed. It is in that moment of eternity that we will finally sing and completely understand the words to that immortal song:

> All hail the power of Jesus' name!
> Let angels prostrate fall;
> Bring forth the royal diadem,
> And crown Him Lord of all.

CHAPTER 10

A Biblical Portrait of the Antichrist

Let no man deceive you by any means: for that day shall not come, except there come a falling away first, and that man of sin be revealed, the son of perdition; who opposeth and exalteth himself above all that is called God, or that is worshipped; so that he as God sitteth in the temple of God, shewing himself that he is God. . . . Even him, whose coming is after the working of Satan with all power and signs and lying wonders (2 Thessalonians 2:3, 4, 9).

And his power shall be mighty, but not by his own power: and he shall destroy wonderfully, and shall prosper, and practise, and shall destroy the mighty and the holy people. And through his policy also he shall cause craft to prosper in his hand; and he shall magnify himself in his heart, and by peace shall destroy man: he shall also stand up against the Prince of princes; but he shall be broken without hand (Daniel 8:24,25).

And every spirit that confesseth not that Jesus Christ is come in the flesh is not of God: and this is that spirit of antichrist, whereof ye have heard that it should come; and even now already is it in the world (I John 4:3).

And all the world wondered after the beast (Revelation 13:3).

The earth and the inhabitants who remain after the Rapture of the church are doomed to a time of unparalleled tragedy. The Bible covers the time of Tribulation in detail, but the reality of the terrible events that take place during that siege of horror is probably beyond imagination. The Nazi death camps of World War II, or the starvation and famine that occurred in Russia during the Bolshevik Revolution, pale in comparison to this approaching tragedy. The blood baths of intertribal warfare as seen in the Congo, or the genocide of Southeast Asia in the '60s and

'70s, give but a taste of the unleashed hell of the Tribulation period.

Before we deal with the events of this approaching era however, it is important to take a look at the central figure that will be responsible for much of the carnage and destruction that will occur during this horrendous time.

Prophecy scholars commonly call this individual the Antichrist. In the Bible, however, a number of additional names or phrases are used to identify or describe him. In Daniel 8:23, he is described as "a king of fierce countenance, and understanding dark sentences." In Zechariah 11:17, he is referred to as the "idol shepherd." In Revelation 6:2, he is seen as a conqueror, armed with a bow, wearing a crown and riding a white horse. In Revelation 13:1-8, he is called "the beast." Paul called him "that man of sin . . . the son of perdition" and also "that Wicked" (2 Thessalonians 2:3, 8). It is noteworthy that all of his names and titles testify to the intense evil of his nature and character. He is truly a child of the devil, and his purpose on the earth is clearly stated by the apostle Paul: "Who opposeth and exalteth himself above all that is called God, or that is worshipped" (2 Thessalonians 2:4).

There are specific conditions that are to exist

in the earth at the time of the Rapture—events that will tell us the stage is being set for the rise of the Antichrist. The Antichrist will have characteristics and personality traits that will appeal to the masses. Through these conditions and events, combined with his appeal to man's nature, multitudes will succumb to his influence. The earth has spent the latter half of the 20th century setting the stage for the tragedy that is to be played out during the Tribulation. Satan himself will produce this apocalypse, but the director will be the Antichrist. When the tragedy is finished, earth will lie in ruins from war, disease, the upheaval of nature, the unlimited wrath of God, and unbridled demonic activity. Only Christ, descending to earth with His army of glorified saints, will be able to redeem this planet and bring a millennial reign of peace.

What has happened for this stage to be set? Let us examine the history of Planet Earth in the latter part of the 20th century, observing key elements that set the stage for the rise of the Man of Sin.

Communication. First of all, every description of the Antichrist—whether given by Daniel, Paul, or John the Revelator—indicates that he is a master of communication. There is a unique element, however, that distinguishes him from other mad despots who happened to be skilled communicators. He will be able to communicate his message to the entire world at the same time. In other words, the world's populace will be able to see and hear him as he performs his deeds, live. This was not possible only a few short years ago. In Revelation 13:3 we read, "And all the world wondered after the beast." In verse 7 the Scripture states, "And power was given him over all kindreds, and tongues, and nations." Verse 8 states, "And all that dwell upon the earth shall worship him, whose names are not written in the book of life of the Lamb slain from the foundation of the world."

The rest of chapter 13 tells of a false prophet who arises as a protégé and spokesman for the Beast. He is a master of deception and satanic trickery. In verse 14 the Bible says that he "deceiveth them that dwell on the earth by the means of those miracles which he had power to do in the sight of the beast."

The bottom line here is that the influence of the Antichrist and his false prophet is not relegated to Israel or a small geographic section of the earth, as some would try to teach. The Bible is very, very plain. This man will mesmerize the entire world (v. 8). The Tribulation will be a time of trial for the entire earth, according to Jesus: "For as a snare shall it come on all them that dwell on the face of the whole earth" (Luke 21:35).

In the late 1940s an electronic media was introduced that would change the world forever. Television came to the world, as the world was recovering from the trauma of World War II. For about 25 years the world had listened to radio. The little boxes of sound were heard in living rooms and general stores around our nation and, in a great measure, had succeeded in reducing the size of the world. By the start of World War II, people could listen to newscasts from around the world. The sounds of sirens during the blitz of London, the bombing of Manila, and the cannons and tanks on the beaches of Normandy were brought into the homes of multiplied thousands.

Television, however, went much further than radio had ever dreamed of. Television put faces and personalities with the voices. News, entertainment, and sports could now be seen as they occurred. America was enchanted with the advent of television. Family meals were interrupted or cut short for favorite programs that just had to be watched. News bulletins stopped everyone in their tracks and eyes were glued to the set.

At first the programming was innocent enough, for we were still a nation of convictions and of a

Judeo-Christian ethic. Light comedy, westerns, police dramas where bad guys always lost, sports by basically clean-cut athletes, and late-breaking news developments made up the spectrum of television offerings to the public. In time, something dreadful happened. Wars, an increasingly violent world, an eroding of moral and ethical codes, the influence of drugs and alcohol, and an anti-Christian agenda embraced by the media empires began to poison television programming. As the television media itself sank in the abyss of moral depravity, all forms of media began to be affected. The late 20th century saw music that appealed to young people, influenced by drugs, alcohol, and, worst of all, by Satanism. Pornography, in all of its vile forms, grew to be an industry generating billions of dollars a year. The Hollywood media machines—through music, movies, television, and printed media—began mass production of anti-Christian, anti-Biblical products that have had a tremendous effect. In our lifetime we have witnessed our society quickly sink from a Judeo-Christian culture to one of agnostic nothingness. There is now a subtle mind-set that has laid hold on the entire world that says, "I am willing to accept anything."

In one respect, this is a great opportunity for

Christians to portray Jesus Christ and preach the gospel to all nations. This accounts for the worldwide revival that is going on today. On the other hand, this revival movement has created an antagonism toward religion in general and Christianity in particular. In fact there are many people in various circles—political, educational, and industrial—who blame religion for the problems of our age. Recently I heard an educated young man in Australia say, "I cannot see where Christianity has any relevance at all in this modern world." His opinions are echoed all over the planet. An educator at a major university that was originally founded as a religious institution stated, "What we don't need now is more young people who feel called to be clergymen."

This cynical viewpoint of Christianity has evolved primarily due to the influence of our media-oriented society. What we see, hear, and experience combine to form our opinions. Unfortunately, televised media provides all of these criteria. Hence, when there are no boundaries and this type of media operates unleashed, we have today's sick society. A larger version of the day of Noah or the day of Lot is what we have become. The people of Noah's day resented and laughed at his righteous preaching, and Lot's sons-in-law mocked him upon hearing of

Sodom's impending doom. In the same way, television and the Hollywood audiovisual media of our day have formed mind-sets and molded opinions with their anti-Christian programming.

Just think of it! A whole generation from birth to adulthood has been molded in opinion and thought by this infamous electronic infiltrator. Parents have employed television as both baby-sitter and nanny. With the advent of the VCR, movies of every nature are at the fingertips of eager watchers. Though much good has been done by sincere Christian television programming, horrible and irreparable damage has been done by some of the televangelists. Their lives became scandal sheets, covered with bogus money scams and sexual immorality. These scandals only added to the cynicism and the erroneous opinion that hypocrisy lies in the heart of all those that present themselves as sincere and passionate Christians. This view of Christianity has helped set the stage for the Antichrist. The spirit that does not want to acknowledge that Jesus Christ is the Son of God and that He has come in the flesh is, according to the apostle John, a "spirit of antichrist" (1 John 4:3).

Late 20th century advances in technology have greatly enhanced television and other forms of communication, further setting the stage for the rise of the Antichrist. Worldwide satellite communications both oral and visual are now totally and completely normative. Major cities of the earth have large-screen satellite reception capabilities. It is technologically possible for everyone on earth—at the same time—to watch an event take place. In fact, Revelation 13 confirms this. In this chapter the Antichrist receives a mortal wound, but miraculously recovers. Here is a genuine miracle done by the power of the devil, for the Bible says this wound was "to death." The whole world obviously witnesses this take place—"All the world wondered after the beast" (v. 3).

In verses 14 and 15, the False Prophet makes an image to the Beast and then causes that image to live. The world is made to worship this image, and those who refuse are killed. One hundred years ago the world could not have seen this. Even before the last few years they could not have seen this. However, it is now possible simply due to technology and televised media.

Worldwide revival of Satanism. Another thing that has set the stage for the rise of the Antichrist has been the recent worldwide revival of Satanism. Much of this has been subtle and silent. The open and loud Satanists are few and have been largely replaced by silent worshipers of the devil who are growing by leaps and bounds. In some European nations the leading religious preference has now become Satanism. Thousands of satanic priests recently responded to a government request in Britain for the registration of religious clergymen. In Belgium, missionaries report that the number one religion in that nation, the headquarters of NATO, is Satanism. Much of northern Europe, and almost half of Germany are now avowed Satanists. In the United States, secret satanic organizations like the Brotherhood have hundreds of thousands of members, boasting of doctors, lawyers, educators, and industry heads. Federal law-enforcement agencies estimate that at least one satanic coven exists in every county and parish in the United States. Music, magazines, movies, and television both openly and subtly extol the benefits of this lifestyle while mocking the virtues of Christianity. An atmosphere is developing. A darkened cloud of tribulation and judgment is looming over the horizon.

Man of Sin. Let us look at what this Man of Sin will be like. What is he about? Phrases the prophets and apostles used in describing him tell us much about his character. Daniel described him as "a king of fierce countenance, and understanding dark sentences" (8:23). He also states that "his power shall be mighty, but not by his own power" (v. 24).

Both of these descriptions speak of a man totally dependent on Satan and given over to demonic control. The words "fierce countenance" denote the aura of satanic power and influence that can be seen in the Antichrist's physical appearance. "Fierce" here denotes the determination, zeal, and rage that drive him to his deeds of ungodly behavior. Daniel's use of the phrase "understanding dark sentences" refers to the Antichrist's occultic ties with the satanic underworld.

Paul's passage in Ephesians 6:12 categorizes the levels of demonic hierarchy that rule on the earth, and it is with these "rulers of the darkness of this world" that the Antichrist will form a league of evil. No wonder occultic activity in the world is at a historical high. No wonder that the forces of darkness have subtly taken over the communications media of the world and have established themselves in the hearts of cynical, agnostic people who laugh at Christianity and mock the values of the Bible. The Antichrist will be a dark, sinister servant of Satan. All students of the Scripture understand and accept the fact that the devil's power is very real indeed. Peter called him "a roaring lion" (1 Peter 5:8). Paul said he transforms himself into "an angel of light" (2 Corinthians 11:14). His very name (Satan) identifies him as an accuser. The Bible says that of his creation he was

166

"full of wisdom, and perfect in beauty" and that because of his sin he became "filled . . . with violence" (Ezekiel 28:12, 16). Jesus said he was a "thief [who came] to steal, and to kill, and to destroy" (John 10:10). Satan's power, wisdom, and totally violent nature are proclaimed in Scripture. Since the Antichrist is the "son of perdition" completely sold out to Satan, we must conclude, according to Daniel 8:24, that Satan will give this man satanic power to accomplish his works.

Paul, too, describes the Antichrist as a man under satanic control. In 2 Thessalonians 2:9, the Apostle to the Gentiles gives us this graphic description: "Even him, whose coming is after the working of Satan with all power and signs and lying wonders." Here is a man who is the epitome of deception. His wonders are "lying wonders." Furthermore, Paul says the Antichrist will totally deceive the unrighteous who refuse to receive the truth in the days before the Rapture. Then God will send "strong delusion" to the people of the earth who are following Antichrist. They will believe his lies and be damned (vv. 10-12).

What a warning to the world! A man of sin will come on the scene of world politics and will deceive the masses of earth as Satan empowers him.

167

In Such an Hour

Satan will empower his personality, and it will be one of unerring charm and deceit. Satan will give him power to bring peace, economic prosperity, and harmony in the Middle East. He will become the beloved, admired, and worshiped leader of the world.

Daniel speaks of his skills of administration as a world leader. In 8:24 we are told he will "practise," which means that he will accomplish or perform his will. The modernization of our present world demands this type of leader, and the Antichrist will not disappoint them. He will not be a slow-witted, dull laggard, but rather a decisive leader who makes calculated, popular decisions, which Satan will enable to work. Daniel, in this same verse, said he "shall prosper." As he rises to power he will be the portrait of prosperity. John said the world will "wonder after the beast" (Revelation 13:3). There will be no jealousy of his attained estate, but instead he will be admired for his accomplishments and looked up to as a man of success who is to be followed without question. Daniel also tells us that the Antichrist will bring about economic prosperity; his governing policies "shall cause craft to prosper" (8:25).

In Revelation 6:2, when the Lamb opens the first seal of the seven-sealed book, the Antichrist is

168

seen in the beginning of his reign of world domination. He is riding a white horse, carrying a bow, and donning a crown on his head. He is hailed as a mighty conqueror. This entire early period of his career is designed to gain the world's trust. It works. The world is soon in his grip.

Where does this futuristic world dictator come from? From what geographic region of the earth does he emerge? Bible and prophecy scholars have debated this question for centuries. God has His divine reasons for not revealing everything, for He knows the true nature of man and uses great wisdom in His revelations to us. However, the earth is really a small place and the origins of the Antichrist can be narrowed down in a very general way.

Daniel 8 is a prophecy of the empires of ancient Greece and ancient Media-Persia. A vision was given to Daniel (vv. 1-14) in which he saw a powerful ram who pushed toward the north, west, and south. This ram had two horns, one higher than the other, and the higher horn grew out of the ram last. As he was watching this ram, he saw a "he goat" coming swiftly from the west. This male goat had one large horn between his eyes. His feet moved so swiftly that they didn't touch the ground. He attacked the ram and destroyed him and became very great. In the height of his power his great horn was broken off. In its place came four smaller horns, and from them came a little horn that became very great and powerful.

Gabriel himself gives Daniel an explanation of this vision and tells him that it relates to the "time of the end" (vv. 16, 17, 20 ff.). The ram represents the kingdom of Media-Persia. Notice the ram had two horns, the higher, or stronger one, coming up last. Media-Persia had two great kings, Darius the Mede and Cyrus the Persian. Darius was an older man and ruled first; Cyrus was younger and became much more powerful. The "he goat" was the nation of Greece and the "great horn" was Alexander the Great. Alexander moved swiftly, just like the male goat, and had conquered the world by age 30. In the height of his power as a very young man, it is said that he died in great sorrow, for he had no more worlds to conquer. When he died his empire was divided among his four great generals: Macedonia to the west, Egypt to the south, Assyria to the east, and Turkey (Asia Minor) to the north. It is out of one of these ancient Grecian divisions that a "little horn" arises.

Some scholars point to the ancient King Antiochus Epiphanes, who arose during this time and persecuted the Jews, even sacrificing a sow on their altar, as a type and shadow of the Antichrist. Others contend that Antiochus was the "little horn." However, the problem in identifying him as such is that the angel Gabriel specifically stated that this prophecy was for the "time of the end" (Daniel 8:17). The best explanation is that perhaps from this area of the globe, the Antichrist will arise. Daniel's prophecy of a "little horn" that arises in the last days, and its similarity to John's vision of the Beast in Revelation 13:1, 2, tells us that the Antichrist will most likely arise from within the boundaries of the old Roman and Greek empires.

As to his identity the Scripture is silent. In fact Paul indicates that the church's presence on this earth prevents his identification from being made public until after the rapture of the church (2 Thessalonians 2:6-8). Speculation has accused many men of being the rising Antichrist. However, such speculation is futile, especially for the Christian. To make positive identification of the Antichrist, one will have to be here after the church is gone and see his rapid rise to power. What we can see is the stage that is being set for his presentation. Every element he needs to glide rapidly to power is being set in place.

The casual observer may think that this is Satan's time and that these are Lucifer's triumphant days. Nothing could be further from the truth. What is going on then? Why are these seven years of the Antichrist's domination the most devastating in all of human history? Answers to these questions can be clearly observed in the cries of dying men who are praying for death while God's judgment is falling. Their cry is heard in Revelation 6:15-17:

> And the kings of the earth, and the great men, and the rich men, and the chief captains, and the mighty men, and every bondman, and every free man, hid themselves in the dens and in the rocks of the mountains; and said to the mountains and rocks, Fall on us, and hide us from the face of him that sitteth on the throne, and from the wrath of the Lamb: For the great day of his wrath is come; and who shall be able to stand?

Chapter 11

"Woe to the Inhabiters of the Earth"

 *For then shall be great tribulation, such as was not since the beginning of the world to this time, no, nor ever shall be* (Matthew 24:21).

For in those days shall be affliction, such as was not from the beginning of the creation which God created unto this time, neither shall be (Mark 13:19).

For as a snare shall it come on all them that dwell on the face of the whole earth (Luke 21:35). *Alas! for that day is great, so that none is like it: it is even the time of Jacob's trouble, but he shall be saved out of it* (Jeremiah 30:7).

And there shall be a time of trouble, such as never was since there was a nation even to that same time (Daniel 12:1).

The sun and the moon shall be darkened, and the stars shall withdraw their shining. The Lord also shall roar out of Zion, and utter his voice from Jerusalem; and the heavens and the earth shall shake (Joel 3:15, 16).

For when they shall say, Peace and safety; then sudden destruction cometh upon them, as travail upon a woman with child; and they shall not escape (1 Thessalonians 5:3).

Tribulation—the word itself reeks with fear and foreboding. *Webster's* dictionary defines *tribulation* as "a state, cause, or instance of affliction or suffering." Humanities history is replete with instances of human suffering. It began on a cool evening in Eden's Garden when the first human pair, the ancestors of us all, heard judgment pronounced because of their sin. Regardless of what ran through their minds that day, there was no way that Adam and Eve could begin to comprehend what sin would do to them and all of their descendants. As they trembled in their fig-leaf coats, they heard God say, "Cursed is the ground for thy sake" (Genesis 3:17). And so the suffering that began as a result of sin ensued.

174

The earth would never be the same. Adam and Eve's oldest son would murder his younger brother. Every sin imaginable would develop in the hearts of men and then would be acted out in their deeds. The cursed ground would see drought, flood, famine, and earthquakes. Suffering, disease, and affliction would plague the human race until it was simply accepted as part of the experience of being an inhabitant of Planet Earth.

Man's entire history since Eden's Garden has been a history of trying to better his predicament in life. His advances in science, medicine, and technology are achievements intended to overcome the trouble he has inherited as a result of his sin.

But what we're about to deal with is a giant leap beyond normal or even cataclysmic human suffering. The Tribulation period that the Bible foretells is so far beyond anything the human race has ever encountered that it defies normal description. Here is catastrophe on a grand scale. The death toll alone, according to the Book of Revelation, will total almost two-thirds of the world's population. Nature will experience an upheaval the likes of which the earth has never known. Unique and totally bizarre events will take place in the spirit world as the devil and his fallen angels are released upon the world and given unlimited and free access to wreak havoc on the earth. Demonic creatures never before seen, except through anointed prophetical eyes, will suddenly appear out of their secret subterranean chambers to inflict pain, torment, suffering, and death upon the human race. The beasts of the earth will be relentless in their pursuit of human flesh. The heavens themselves will pelt the earth with projectiles and poison, as blood and death pollute earth's seas and rivers.

To understand all of this, it is necessary to analyze the Tribulation period in the various categories of judgment that are to descend.

Chronological. First, let us deal with the time frame of the Tribulation. For simplicity's sake, please note that we are talking about the time period between the rapture of the church and the visible return of Christ and the saints back to the earth to set up His millennial reign of peace. Most Bible scholars calculate that this period of time will last for seven years. That time frame is derived from Daniel's prophecy of 70 weeks:

> Seventy weeks are determined upon thy people and upon the holy city, to finish the transgression, and to make an end of sins,

and to make reconciliation for iniquity, and to bring in everlasting righteousness, and to seal up the vision and prophecy, and to anoint the most Holy. Know therefore and understand, that from the going forth of the commandment to restore and to rebuild Jerusalem unto the Messiah the Prince shall be seven weeks, and threescore and two weeks: the street shall be built again, and the wall, even in troublous times. And after threescore and two weeks shall Messiah be cut off, but not for himself: and the people of the prince that shall come shall destroy the city and the sanctuary; and the end thereof shall be with a flood, and unto the end of the war desolations are determined. And he shall confirm the covenant with many for one week: and in the midst of the week he shall cause the sacrifice and the oblation to cease, and for the overspreading of abominations he shall make it desolate, even until the consummation, and that determined shall be poured upon the desolate (Daniel 9:24-27).

Now the reader must realize that the original

language translated here as "seventy weeks" literally means "seventy sevens." The Hebrew word for *week* is *"shabuwa,"* meaning "seven." This means we are dealing with 70 sevens of years. Daniel's prayer in chapter 9, to which this vision was an answer, did not concern days but years (v. 2). The last seven-year period is divided into two parts of 3 ½ years each, according to verse 27. So we are dealing with "seventy weeks" of years, or 70 x 7. That calculates to 490 years of Biblical prophecy in Daniel 9:24-27.

Now, the first portion of this prophecy, according to verse 25, is 7 sevens, or 49 years for the rebuilding of Jerusalem. The second part is 62 sevens, or 434 years from the completion of the rebuilding of Jerusalem to the time the Messiah is "cut off," or crucified. This leaves 7 years for the things that are prophesied in verse 24 to take place. God told Daniel that 490 years, or 70 "weeks," were determined upon His people Israel. From the time that the commandment went forth to rebuild Jerusalem until Jesus was crucified, 483 years transpired, or 69 of Daniel's 70 "weeks." This leaves 7 years, or the 70th week of Daniel's prophecy yet to be fulfilled.

In verse 26, Daniel prophesied that after the Messiah had been "cut off" (crucified), a "prince" would come who would destroy the city of Jerusalem and the sanctuary. Titus, the Roman general, did this in A.D. 70, approximately 35 years after Jesus' death. Titus, however, was not the fulfillment of the leader spoken of in verse 27 who would confirm the covenant with Israel and bring about the abomination of desolation. Verse 27 must be fulfilled in the 70th week, or the last seven years of the prophecy.

Verse 24 tells us that six things will be done during this 70th week. First, "to finish the transgression" refers to the conversion of Israel to their true Messiah and the belief in Him that will put an end to their sins. Second, "to make an end of sins" means that a spirit of repentance will be poured out upon Israel just before the Second Advent. Zechariah 12:10 says, "And I will pour upon the house of David, and upon the inhabitants of Jerusalem, the spirit of grace and of supplications: and they shall look upon me whom they have pierced, and they shall mourn for him, as one mourneth for his only son." Third, "to make reconciliation for iniquity" means to cover or make atonement. As a nation they will be reconciled to God at the Second Advent. Fourth, "to bring in everlasting righteousness" is something that will happen due to this acceptance of the true Messiah. The last two things during this week will be "to seal

179

up the vision and prophecy" and "to anoint the most Holy." These events will all concern the nation of Israel and the Jewish acceptance of Christ. A great catalyst for this will be the relationship they will have with the Antichrist, which will sour and turn violent during the Tribulation.

This is why the Tribulation is often referred to as 3 ½ years of "lesser tribulation" and 3 ½ years of "greater tribulation." You might ask the question, Why is there a gap between the 69th week and the 70th week in Daniel's prophecy? This gap is the era we refer to as the church age, God's time for the church's mission on this earth. Notice the words of Jesus in Matthew 24:14: "And this gospel of the kingdom shall be preached in all the world for a witness unto all nations; and then shall the end come." This is a portrait of the church fulfilling the Great Commission (Matthew 28:19, 20). When this mission is over, Daniel's Seventieth Week will begin, initiating the most horrible seven years of all time.

Political/Economic. Second, let us consider the political and financial judgments upon the earth. Governmental structures in various forms currently rule the nations of the earth. The modernization of the world has caused an interdependence of all nations of the earth upon each other. Global commerce in all of its forms has created a very fragile economic system that can rise and fall in a matter of minutes depending upon world conditions. War, natural disaster, variations in supply and demand of products, and political upheaval all play their roles in the fluctuation of our world's economy. Isolationism is a phenomenon of the past that can no longer meet the needs of a nation. North Korea is a prime example of this. Their political isolation has brought them famine and national poverty that has led them to the brink of war or internal destruction.

One thing that will help propel the Antichrist into the world's spotlight will probably be the Rapture itself. The world will undoubtedly be momentarily traumatized by the Rapture. Something will probably happen to divert the attention of the world away from the event that has just taken place. Certainly a nuclear holocaust or major war would do this. Since according to Daniel 8 and Revelation 6, the Antichrist rises to power promising peace, there must be a state of war or international unrest. The Antichrist's promise of peace, however, is merely a ploy, for he will use "peace [to] destroy many" (Daniel 8:25).

Many Biblical scholars point to the Battle of Gog and Magog that Ezekiel prophesied in chapters

38 and 39. In this battle, forces from the north, descendants of the ancient Scynthians and Muscovites, descend upon Israel in great numbers. They are accompanied by their allies from Persia (modern Iran), Ethiopia, and Libya (Ezekiel 38:5). All of the enemies' names are significant. The enemies of the north—Magog, Meshech, Tubal, Gomer, and Togarmah (38:2, 6)—are all descendants of Noah's son Japheth (Genesis 10:2). These peoples settled from Galatia and Phrygia to modern Russia and Germany—in the areas of Iberia, Georgia, and Cappadocia. Geographically, this is the region where most of the old southern extremities of the former Soviet Union are located.

Most of these people are followers of Islam. United with Iran, Ethiopia, and Libya, they form a vast army of sworn Islamic enemies of Israel. They will descend on the mountains of Israel and here God himself will put "hooks in their jaws" and slay them (Ezekiel 38:4). God said they will "come like a storm" and will "be like a cloud," covering the land (v. 9).

The Bible also mentions allies of Israel who will rise up in protest against this attack. Ezekiel 38:13 refers to "Sheba, and Dedan, and the merchants of Tarshish, with all the young lions thereof." Some scholars believe that "the merchants of Tarshish" is a reference to the British Isles and the "young lions" are young powerful nations which have emerged from Great Britain. If these assumptions are correct, a reasonable argument could be offered that the United States, Canada, Australia, and New Zealand (all young nations formed from British colonies) will rise up to protest this attack upon Israel.

It is entirely possible that this attack on Israel, prophesied in Ezekiel, will occur in close proximity to the rapture of the church. The Bible says that the house of Israel will burn the weapons from this battle for seven years (39:9). This seven-year time line is very important, for it corresponds with the established length of the Tribulation period. This battle will also provide a sound platform for the Antichrist to arise, promising peace to a world and nation at war. Of course this is all speculation, but good speculation is built on sound reason. Regardless of what is going on, the Antichrist will rise to power and the world will be in awe at his presence.

For the Antichrist to arise promising economic prosperity (Daniel 8:25), there must be a time of economic panic. A sudden global war or an upsetting world event like the rapture of the church could throw the global economy into a state of high anxiety. If this were coupled with natural disasters like famine, hurricanes, earthquakes, and floods, one could readily see the awesome consequences.

The Bible is explicit in its description of the economic chaos and depression that will reign on the earth during the Tribulation. In Revelation 6:5, a third horseman is revealed, who signifies another dimension of the Tribulation period. He is riding a black horse and has a pair of scales in his hand. A voice provides an explanation for what is happening at this stage of the Tribulation. John records, "And I heard a voice in the midst of the four beasts say, A measure of wheat for a penny, and three measures of barley for a penny; and see thou hurt not the oil and the wine" (v. 6). The black horse represents famine, which has come to the earth as a result of the conflict and war brought on by the first two horsemen, riding the white and the red horses respectively (vv. 2, 4). Bread sold by weight and measure represents a scarcity of this precious commodity. The word *penny* as used here means "a day's wages," and the measure of wheat or barley it could buy is the exact measure rationed to a slave in the days of the New Testament. Both the olive and the grape need little cultivation, and both wine from the grapes and oil from the olives can be kept for long periods of time, therefore their destruction is forbidden. All of these symbolize a worldwide famine.

A man will have to work all day for a handful of bread. Consider the billions who inhabit this planet and the small percentage of land suitable for growing food. Consider also how natural disasters can destroy crops by the billions of tons and that nuclear war could do even greater damage. The probability of worldwide famine becomes obvious. God said it; it will happen.

The financial structure of the world will rapidly change during the Tribulation period. Already, in this computerized age, we are swiftly heading toward a cashless society. The Bible tells us that when the Antichrist reaches the zenith of his power, he will institute a financial system in which "he causeth all, both small and great, rich and poor, free and bond, to receive a mark in their right hand, or in their foreheads: and that no man might buy or sell, save he that had the mark, or the name of the beast, or the number of his name" (Revelation 13:16, 17).

Computerized technology now makes this possible. The capability exists to record the names and pertinent biographical and financial information of every person on Planet Earth in a single database system. A readable mark permanently imprinted in

the skin could then be computer-scanned, determin-
ing the worth or debt of an individual in seconds.
Purchases would be deducted or credit added to the
person's numbered account through the same
system. Just a few years ago, this was unimaginable.
Today it is not only imaginable but also likely. It
will be done once the structure and organization are
set in place.

This system will give the Antichrist and his
government electronic control over all the earth. Of
course, violations will occur and there will be people
who refuse to take the mark. Their sentence will be
immediate death. According to John's vision, they
will turn to Christ after the Rapture and die as martyrs rather than receive the mark and worship the
Antichrist. John said:

> And I saw thrones, and they sat upon them,
> and judgment was given unto them: and I
> saw the souls of them that were beheaded
> for the witness of Jesus, and for the word
> of God, and which had not worshipped the
> beast, neither his image, neither had received
> his mark upon their foreheads, or in their
> hands; and they lived and reigned with Christ
> a thousand years (Revelation 20:4).

Revelation 13:18 tells us the number of the Antichrist. Though we are not told what his mark is exactly, we are told the number of the Beast. This means literally the total number of his name. We are told this number is "the number of a man." In the Greek and Hebrew alphabets, letters are also used for numbers, unlike the English alphabet where letters are simply put together to form words that spell numbers. The Greek and Hebrew letters are in themselves a system of numbers, and there are many Greek and Hebrew names that have a numerical value of "666." This is indeed a mystery, for this is the numerical value of so many names, and we still do not know what the mark will be. No true Christian wants this knowledge, however, for it can only be gained after the rapture of the church. It will be learned in horror.

Devastation. Third, the plagues that will beset the world during the Tribulation are many. Together, they paint a portrait of a dark and turmoil-filled hour. Revelation 16 tells us of seven angels of judgment, who will pour out vials of God's wrath upon the earth. The first angel will pour out his vial, and horrible ulcerating sores will plague the men of earth (v. 2). The second angel's vial will be poured out, and the seas will become as "the blood of a dead man" (v. 3). Every living thing in the sea will die. The stench of decomposing blood will fill the earth's air. The third angel will pour out his vial upon the rivers and fountains of waters, and they will also become blood, contaminating the fresh drinking water of earth (v. 4).

The fourth angel will pour his vial upon the sun, and it will erupt with great heat, scorching those on earth (v. 8). This is not beyond the bounds of reason, for we know that the sun is a burning gaseous star and it is volatile at best. In the Tribulation it will begin to deviate from normality.

The fifth angel will pour out his vial, and darkness will cover the Antichrist's kingdom. Men will gnaw their tongues for pain, and will blaspheme God because of their sores and refuse to repent of their evil deeds (vv. 10, 11). The sixth angel will pour out his vial in the Middle East, and the great river Euphrates will dry up. The kings of Asia will then be able to march toward Armageddon (v. 12). John saw three demons that will come forth from the Dragon (devil), the Beast (Antichrist), and the False Prophet. These will "go forth unto the kings of the earth and of the whole world, to gather them to the battle of that great day of God Almighty" (vv. 13, 14).

The seventh angel will pour out his vial into

the air and will cry out, "It is done" (v. 17). Immediately, heaven will be filled with voices, thunder, and lightning. The greatest earthquake in history will shake the entire world. Jerusalem will be divided into three parts. World governments will fall and tremble under the fierceness of God's wrath. The islands of the earth will disappear and mountains will be leveled. Hailstones weighing a talent each, or about 60-100 pounds, will begin to pelt the earth. The devastation caused by all of this will be beyond imagination (vv. 18-21).

The collapse of cities, towns, villages, hamlets, and homes alone will mean the death of millions. Power lines, oil and gas depositories, chemical factories, world communication, hospitals, emergency services, and water supplies will all be demolished and destroyed. This is but a small glimpse of what will occur in the fulfillment of Revelation 16.

Revelation 18 tells of worldwide anguish that will take place because of the fall of "Babylon the great." Many believe this refers to a world economic and governmental system of international cooperation during the Tribulation. The governmental world will lament her fall (vv. 9, 10). The commercial world, representing world merchandising and money, will mourn her passing (vv. 12-16). The maritime world that rules the seas will bemoan the fall of Babylon (vv. 17-19). The main thrust of Revelation 18 is that all will be crumbling and falling. Modern man's pride in his empire of power and treasure will then be realized as complete and utter vanity. In a moment's time under God's wrath, it will crumble.

As the Tribulation unwinds and Armageddon looms on the horizon, the earth will be left in smoking ruins. The animals of the earth, frightened out of their wits by the upheavals of nature, will become vicious killers and will hunt and slay thousands (Revelation 6:8). Men will be tormented by demonic creatures called "locusts" that will not kill but will inflict such pain that men will beg to die (9:3-6). Wars will have been continual and blood will have flowed freely. The world will be a cauldron of despair.

Certainly nuclear explosions and catastrophes will occur. Zechariah 14:12 states, "Their flesh shall consume away while they stand upon their feet, and their eyes shall consume away in their holes, and their tongues shall consume away in their mouth." Peter declared, "The heavens shall pass away with a great noise, and the elements shall melt with fervent heat, the earth also and the works that are therein shall be burned up" (2 Peter 3:10). This ancient Hebrew prophet and this fervent New Testament apostle both lived thousands of years before the advent of nuclear weapons, yet their descriptions of last-days events vividly and accurately describe the outcome of nuclear calamity. The inspiration of the Holy Spirit once more demonstrates God's eternal foreknowledge of all things.

As it was stated in the beginning of this chapter, the Tribulation period is almost indescribable, but we have ventured to briefly look at this time of sorrow. When I was a lad, an old hymn of conviction and judgment was often sung in my church. It has been years since I have heard it sung, and most of the words, shrouded in the midst of time, have escaped my memory. However, I can still clearly hear the chorus of "The Great Judgment Morning" and remember as a little boy how it made me think of eternity:

> And oh, what a weeping and wailing,
> As the lost were told of their fate;
> They cried for the rocks and the mountains,
> They prayed, but their prayer was too late.
> —Rev. Bert Shadduck

Chapter 12

THE RETURN AND JUDGMENT

 *Behold, he cometh with clouds; and every eye shall see him, and they also which pierced him: and all kindreds of the earth shall wail because of him. Even so, Amen* (Revelation 1:7).

And I saw heaven opened, and behold a white horse; and he that sat upon him was called Faithful and True, and in righteousness he doth judge and make war. His eyes were as a flame of fire, and on his head were many crowns; and he had a name written, that no man knew, but he himself. And he was clothed with a vesture dipped in blood: and his name is called The Word of God. And the armies which were in heaven followed him upon white horses, clothed in fine linen, white and clean. And out of his mouth goeth a sharp sword, that with it he should smite the nations: and he shall rule them

with a rod of iron: and he treadeth the winepress of the fierceness and wrath of Almighty God. And he hath on his vesture and on his thigh a name written, KING OF KINGS, AND LORD OF LORDS (19:11-16).

And I saw a great white throne, and him that sat on it, from whose face the earth and the heaven fled away; and there was found no place for them. And I saw the dead, small and great, stand before God; and the books were opened: and another book was opened, which is the book of life: and the dead were judged out of those things which were written in the books, according to their works. . . . And whosoever was not found written in the book of life was cast into the lake of fire (20:11, 12, 15).

When the Biblical prophecies concerning that cataclysmic time have taken place, the Tribulation itself will end in a whirlpool of blood and death. By the end of the seven years of Tribulation, according to the Word of God, the earth will be in a state of total and complete chaos. Nature will have gone berserk. Seas and rivers will have become polluted. Rampaging wild beasts will have devoured many. Powerful earthquakes, meteor showers, and sudden changes in the sun and moon will have taken place. The plagues of nature and worldwide war, coupled with the effects of nuclear explosions, will have taken a horrible toll (see Zechariah 14:12; 2 Peter 3:10).

By the end of the Tribulation, Israel will have recognized the Antichrist for his falsehood and will have turned to Jesus as their Messiah. During the Tribulation, 144,000 Jews will have had the seal of God placed in their forehead, which will protect them from the trumpet judgments that will begin in chapter 8 (Revelation 7:3, 4).

In Revelation 11 we are told of two witnesses who will arise during the Tribulation period. They will have the power to devour their enemies (v. 5). They will be able to turn water into blood and smite the earth with plagues as often as they will (v. 6). They will prophesy as Christ's witnesses the last 3 1/2 years of the Tribulation (v. 3).

We are not told explicitly the identity of these two witnesses, but a careful study of related texts will enable us to make a reasonable assumption. God tells John that they will be "two olive trees, and . . . two candlesticks standing before the God of the earth" (11:4). This is a clear reference to the vision and prophecy given to Zechariah (ch. 4) in which he saw two olive branches and two golden candlesticks, which represent "the two anointed ones, that stand by the Lord of the whole earth" (v. 14). These two witnesses were already in heaven when Zechariah gave this prophecy approximately 500 years before Christ. This would effectively rule out every man who lived since that time. Since it is "appointed unto men once to die" (Hebrews 9:27), they are obviously men who have never died. They are not immortal, for they die at the end of their days of prophecy (Revelation 11:7). We are told in 2 Kings 2:11 that Elijah was taken alive into heaven by a whirlwind. In Malachi 4:5, 6 we are told that Elijah will return prior to the "great and dreadful day of the Lord." Enoch was the only other man to have escaped death and, like Elijah, was taken alive into heaven (Genesis 5:24; Hebrews 11:5). In view of these Biblical facts, it is reasonable and logical to assume that Enoch and Elijah will be these Tribulation witnesses.

When they have completed their witness, the Antichrist will make war on them and kill them (Revelation 11:7). These witnesses will be so hated by the people of the earth that they will rejoice and make merry over their death, sending gifts to one another in celebration (v. 10). Their bodies will be allowed to remain in the streets of Jerusalem for 3 1/2 days, and then a miracle of vast proportion will take place. They will be brought to life and will

ascend into heaven. As they ascend, another earthquake will happen, destroying a tenth of Jerusalem
(vv. 11-13).

There is little doubt that it will be the preaching of those two witnesses and their ascension that
will turn many in Israel to Christ. In Revelation 12
we are told of John's vision of the sun-clothed woman,
with the moon under her feet and a crown of 12 stars
on her head (v. 1). Sound Biblical reasoning will
lead us to the conclusion that this woman is symbolic of Israel. Israel is very often referred to in Scripture as a woman. In Isaiah 54, God refers to Israel as
a "married wife" and calls Himself Israel's "husband."
In Jeremiah 3:1-14, God illustrates that backslidden
Israel was as a wayward wife gone into adultery. In
Hosea 2:14-23, God specifically refers to Israel with
the feminine pronoun "her." In Joseph's dream in
Genesis 37:9, He shows Israel symbolized by the
sun, moon, and stars.

In the vision of national Israel in Revelation
12, Israel will give birth to a "man child," or a son
(v. 5). This "man child" has been interpreted in a
number of ways. Some speculate that this refers to
the 144,000 of Revelation 7. Others contend that
this refers to Jesus Christ the Messiah. We do know
that both Christ and the saints will rule the earth

together in the millennial reign (Psalm 149:5-9; Revelation 19:1-15). After the birth of the man-child, the devil will try to destroy the nation of Israel, along with the 144,000 sealed saints (12:13-17). Israel will flee into the wilderness and will be protected by God for 3 1/2 years (v. 14). A number of Old Testament prophets prophesied that Israel would be protected during this time in the regions of the ancient kingdoms of Ammon, Moab, and Edom. Psalms 60 and 108, Isaiah 16, Ezekiel 20, Daniel 11, and Hosea 2 all predict the salvation of Israel in the wilderness area of ancient Palestine.

Israel's part in the Tribulation period is prominent, for it is in this geographical area of the world that the end of the Tribulation will take place. Revelation 16:16 reads: "And he gathered them together into a place called in the Hebrew tongue Armageddon." The name means "Mount Meggido," which is on the south side of the Valley of Meggido, or Valley of Esdraelon. This is the entrance to a pass across the Carmel mountain range and is the main passageway between Asia and Africa. This valley has been a battlefield for centuries. One of the greatest pharaohs in Egyptian history, Thutmose III, said, "Meggido is worth a thousand cities!" It will be in this vast valley, as far as the eye can see, that the armies of earth will gather to fight the final battle.

Revelation 19 portrays the Antichrist and the "kings of the earth, and their armies, gathered together to make war against him that sat on the horse, and against his army" (v. 19). What will happen on that occasion can only be explained with both a natural and supernatural understanding. First of all, when Christ literally returns to the earth at the end of the seven-year Tribulation period, He will be visually observed as He returns. Revelation 1:7 says, "Every eye shall see him." The same verse shares with us the fear and foreboding that the people of earth will feel: "And all kindreds of the earth shall wail because of him." This will be both a natural and supernatural phenomenon. With their physical eyes the populace of earth will see the shining bright figure of Christ descending from heaven. Behind Him will be a multitude that no man can number, clothed in bright white linen, riding white horses. This great multitude will be shouting "Alleluia: for the Lord God omnipotent reigneth" (19:6, 11-14). This shout of the redeemed saints will resound like deep thunder from the heavens. Men and women who have been mired in ungodliness and debauchery, and whose souls have been sold out to the devil, will grip their weapons tightly with their marked palms and prepare themselves for war against this heavenly invasion.

The sight of Christ leading this army is one the universe will never forget. The Creator will return to His creation and will find it ruined and contaminated with the stench and filth of millenniums of sin. Those who have refused His redemptive plan of salvation and have embraced the "doctrines of devils" will await Him on a Middle Eastern battlefield with swords and clenched teeth.

When Christ came to earth the first time, He arrived as a newborn babe, dependent upon His mother. His tiny eyes opened to the sight of a stable, while His tiny nostrils were filled with the scent of hay and farm animals. Small ears heard the lowing of oxen and the bleating of sheep, animals He himself had created; for "all things were made by him; and without him was not any thing made that was made" (John 1:3). He lived in poverty, was betrayed by friends, and was despised by religious partisans within His own religious and cultural circle. The most powerful government on earth had Him executed with common criminals, in the prime of His earthly ministry. Death claimed the body of the God-man, but death would not make the final pronouncement over Him. God had declared the surety of His resurrection (see Acts 2:27).

On that day, Christ will return to earth again. But what the nations of earth will see will not be the tiny infant of Christmas, though He will be the same Jesus who was once in that stable in Bethlehem; they will see a mighty Conqueror, riding on a celestial snow-white steed. He will come in righteousness to judge and make war (Revelation 19:11). Isaiah saw Him and gave his witness of that day (63:1-4). He saw Him coming out of the wilderness wearing garments dyed like those from Bozrah, an Edomite city where garments were dyed a bright red. Verse 1 says that He will be "glorious in his apparel, travelling in the greatness of his strength." The Messiah identified Himself to the prophet as "I that speak in righteousness, mighty to save" (v. 1). When the prophet inquired as to the reason His garments were red and purple like those of a man treading grapes, the Messiah answered with a statement of judgment: "For I will tread them in mine anger, and trample them in my fury; and their blood shall be sprinkled upon my garments, and I will stain all my raiment. For the day of vengeance is in mine heart, and the year of my redeemed is come" (vv. 3, 4).

The Christ who will descend to earth leading a powerful, untouchable army will have eyes like a flame of fire, a multicrowned head, and a name known only to Himself. His vesture will be dipped in blood, and from His mouth will go a sharp sword. This will represent the power of His spoken word, for Paul declared in 2 Thessalonians 2:8 that Christ will destroy, or "consume," the Antichrist with the "spirit of his mouth." His name will be called "The Word of God," according to Revelation 19:13. Here we are reminded of John's declaration, "In the beginning was the Word, and the Word was with God, and the Word was God" (John 1:1).

The prophet Zechariah wrote concerning Christ's descent:

> Then shall the Lord go forth, and fight against those nations, as when he fought in the day of battle. And his feet shall stand in that day upon the mount of Olives, which is before Jerusalem on the east, and the mount of Olives shall cleave in the midst thereof toward the east and toward the west, and there shall be a very great valley; and half of the mountain shall remove toward the north, and half of it toward the south (14:3, 4).

Imagine, if you will, the power of Christ's literal descent to this earth at the Second Advent. The feet that were once pierced by cruel spikes and fastened to a cross will then touch the Mount of Olives, where He had wept over Jerusalem, and that ancient mountain will split in half like a melon split with a knife. A great valley will form, running from north to south.

The battle that King Jesus and His army will fight will be quick and devastatingly decisive. In Revelation 19:17, the Bible says a great angel will stand where the sun is shining and will cry with a loud voice to all of the carrion-eating fowls that fly in the midst of heaven. These birds who subsist on dead flesh will be invited to "eat the flesh of kings, and the flesh of captains, and the flesh of mighty men . . . and the flesh of all men, both free and bond, both small and great" (v. 18). The Antichrist and his false prophet will then be "cast alive into a lake of fire burning with brimstone" (v. 20). Their deception of the nations will be over, and their end will be eternity in hell. The remnant of his army will then be slain with the sword from Christ's mouth. Whether it will be the chilling shrillness of His cry of vengeance or His command for them to die that will slay them, we do not know. But we do know His Word will slay them (v. 21). What had begun as a dream for many will become ashes and decay. Their twisted, sin-sick minds longed for a world free from God's plan of redemption and moral discipline. Their lust for power and pleasure consumed their thinking, and they welcomed a leader who led them down a primrose path of sensual, carnal possibilities. The rewards of all of this will then be visited upon them.

Their actual demise will begin years earlier when they allow carnal thinking to draw them away from God and the teachings of His Word. They will miss the Rapture because of unregenerate hearts, and any hope for eternal life will be taken away. Their world of technology, skillfully developed by minds God gave them to glorify and use for Him, will create an environment where the rise of the Antichrist will be a natural progression of events. They will have a cashless society, where impregnated marks in the skin, easily scanned by computers, will seem like the logical step toward world peace. With no one buying or selling without the mark, and everyone's actual wealth stored in a central banking system, the world will be free of the crimes of theft. The class structure that has stymied the world will be over under the Antichrist's rule. Rich and poor, small and great—all will be treated the same in the kingdom of the Beast.

The men of the Antichrist's kingdom will also

be deceived by the instability created by the rapture of the church and the myriad of questions that will ensue. This charming man of power and sophistication will quickly abate these fears and anxieties, however. His programs and policies will be masterpieces of administrative expertise. The whole world will quickly accept him. Oh, there will be the "religious fanatics," who will weep without ceasing and will seem to be possessed of a knowledge no one else will have or can believe in the light of all the instant prosperity and peace. They will refuse to follow like everybody else. They will have to be eliminated, and they will be. They will not be able to see the benefits of the marked and perfect world the Antichrist will create. Israel will turn against the Man of Sin and will decide that Jesus is the Messiah they were looking for. All the centuries of pent-up hatred for Israel by non-Christians and anti-Semitists will be unleashed, and Israel again will flee for their lives.

Armageddon will effectively end the Tribulation period. It will be time to rebuild, but one more important thing must first be taken care of. The antagonist of it all, the devil himself, will have to be dealt with. For eons of time he has been at war with God. Since his fall he has filled the universe with sadness and tears. Destroyed lives, shattered dreams, and utter confusion lie in his tracks wherever he has walked. He sowed the seed of sin in Eden's Garden. He filled the heart of Cain with jealousy and hatched the murder of Abel in that fevered brain. He caused Lot to look longingly toward Sodom. He titillated David's eyes with lust for Bathsheba. He filled the hearts of Ananias and Sapphira to cause them to lie to the Holy Ghost. He incited the mob to stone Stephen. He filled the heart of Demas with a love for this present world. He has saturated the world with deceit, hatred, witchcraft, greed, and avarice since time began, but Revelation 20 spells his inevitable doom.

His doom will be twofold and totally under the control and will of God. Immediately after Armageddon, John says that an angel will "come down from heaven, having the key of the bottomless pit and a great chain in his hand" (Revelation 20:1). This mighty angel will literally take hold of the devil and bind him with this chain and cast him into a bottomless pit for a thousand years. The Greek word for *bottomless* is *abussos,* which means "unfathomed, enormous, immeasurable depth."

One might be tempted to ask here why God doesn't just destroy the devil outright. Why will He bind him for a thousand years and then loose him again? The answer is simple: It takes more power to control something than it does to destroy it. As a final testimony to the ages, God will demonstrate who is in control. The celestial hands of Deity will never touch the Serpent. One of God's messengers, a holy angel, will be given the task of divine jailer. Satan will be incarcerated. No wonder the world will have a thousand years of peace—a thousand years without a devil. Peace will come, because the Prince of Peace will reign.

There will be a remnant of earth's population who will survive the Tribulation. They and their descendants will be people whom the righteous saints shall rule over. One can only speculate as to the nature of their survival. Perhaps they will be in far-flung regions, or maybe their own ingenuity and refusal to take the mark of the Beast will save them. They will first miss the Rapture, but will survive the Tribulation and become subservient people to the redeemed during the thousand-year millennial reign of Christ. Unfortunately, some of these people will be deceived by the devil when he is loosed from the bottomless pit.

Along with these survivors of Tribulation, saints of God who returned victoriously with Christ will inhabit the earth. Also, there will be the people who were beheaded during the Tribulation for their refusal to take the mark. These also will be resurrected and will live with Christ on the earth for 1,000 years (Revelation 20:4).

At the end of the thousand years, Satan will be loosed for a season and will once again be allowed to tempt the hearts of men. It is important to understand that the devil will not be able to deceive anyone who had part in the first resurrection. The Bible says in Revelation 20:6 that upon these saints "the second death hath no power." Satan will, however, deceive a number of the people of the world who are descendants of Tribulation survivors. According to verse 8, he will deceive people from "the four quarters of the earth." His chief area of strength will come from Gog and Magog, the geographic region we know as Russia. His army now will be "as the sand of the sea" (v. 8).

What will happen next is swift and sure. They will attack Jerusalem, the capital from which Christ will reign. Though they will surround the camp of the saints and the beloved city, a fire will come down from God out of heaven and devour them (v. 9).

The devil will then be taken and eternally confined to "the lake of fire and brimstone, where the beast and the false prophet are" (v. 10). Here the unholy trinity will forever be tormented together. The devil wants to be God. The Antichrist will want to be the world's savior, and the False Prophet will want to demonstrate his mighty power. Their wills will be destroyed by the majestic power of God. Let no one be deceived. Jesus meant exactly what He said when He declared, "All power is given unto me in heaven and in earth" (Matthew 28:18). The power of God will triumph over all that is evil and sinful. Lucifer's war of retribution will be over for all eternity. The "Lamb of God, which taketh away the sin of the world" (John 1:29) will have done exactly that.

Every detail of futuristic events is not known nor even prophesied about. Some things are for the mind of God only. When Paul was writing his second letter to the Corinthian church, he told of an instance where he was "caught up to the third heaven" and saw things and "heard unspeakable words, which it is not lawful for a man to utter" (2 Corinthians 12:1-4). John heard seven thunders utter something and then was commanded to seal up what he had heard (Revelation 10:4). Paul said, "For we know in part, and we prophesy in part" (1 Corinthians 13:9).

We do not know everything about the future, but we take comfort in the words of Simon Peter: "Nevertheless we, according to his promise, look for new heavens and a new earth, wherein dwelleth righteousness" (2 Peter 3:13).

Chapter 13

EPILOGUE

Every chapter in this book could probably have become a book in and of itself. In fact volumes have been written on the subjects of the Rapture, the Antichrist, the Tribulation, and the Second Advent. This treatise was given, not as a detailed, all-inclusive account of end-time events, but rather as a warning from God to stir the mind and heart of the reader. If upon examining this work you are constrained of the Spirit to search the Scripture, then I will be pleased. If searching the Scripture compels you to examine your life, I will feel rewarded. If after you examine your life, you find yourself lacking in those spiritual virtues that please God, and you experience a personal revival and powerful renewal of your walk with God, then my most earnest hopes will have been realized.

Perhaps this book should not end without looking once more at those things that will happen after the final verdict has been rendered upon the devil. In Revelation 20:11, 12, John foresees God sitting upon The Great White Throne, and the dead, small and great, will stand before Him. Books (and the word here is plural) will be opened which contain the works that men have done, "and the dead [will be] judged out of those things . . . written in the books." Death and hell will deliver up their dead for judgment before this Great White Throne, and their works will be evaluated and judged (v. 13).

There will be no lawyers or barristers to plead anyone's case. There will be no deals struck. Plea bargaining will not occur, and lenient sentences will be unheard of. The Bible is plain: "And whosoever was not found written in the book of life was cast into the lake of fire" (Revelation 20:15).

The generation that has evolved in the latter years of the 20th century is one that believes "there's always an alternative." Their cry is, "We don't want reality, for our fantasy lifestyle has convinced us there's always a way out." The world has even fantasized a God who never judges, who is always benevolent and will never seek vengeance. For many, feel-good religion replaces accountability and there are no cries of repentance. Church growth has become numerical, financial, and structural, but never spiritual. The Lord will return "in such an hour."

On a mountain filled with olive trees, slightly northeast of Jerusalem, across the Kidron Valley, the Carpenter from Nazareth sat in the shade with a group of 12 men. His death and the end of His earthly ministry were imminent. Soon He would be sitting at the right hand of the Father, interceding for those who call upon His name. He knew—though His death, resurrection, and return to the Father were nearing—that He would return again one day. This fact was part of God's eternal plan. But that fact could not be conveyed to these 12 men—and indeed, to men of all time—without a stern warning. His voice, laced with the accent of Galilee, spoke with stern compassion that day: "Therefore be ye also ready: for in such an hour as ye think not the Son of man cometh" (Matthew 24:44).

The warning has been delivered.